Siege of Bryan's Station
and
The Battle of Blue Licks

The Memorial wall erected by the Lexington Chapter D.A.R. around the spring in Bryan's Station, from which the women and girls got water during the siege

Siege of Bryan's Station
and
The Battle of Blue Licks

Warfare on the Kentucky Frontier Between
Settlers and the British & Their Loyalist,
Indian & Renegade Allies, 1782

Reuben T. Durrett
Bennett H. Young
Henry T. Stanton
George W. Ranck

LEONAUR

Siege of Bryan's Station and The Battle of Blue Licks
Warfare on the Kentucky Frontier Between Settlers and the British
& Their Loyalist, Indian & Renegade Allies, 1782
by Reuben T. Durrett
Bennett H. Young
Henry T. Stanton
George W. Ranck

First published in
The Filson Publications Volume 12

Leonaur is an imprint of Oakpast Ltd

Copyright in this form © 2011 Oakpast Ltd

ISBN: 978-0-85706-679-4 (hardcover)
ISBN: 978-0-85706-680-0 (softcover)

http://www.leonaur.com

Publisher's Notes

Contents

The First Act in the Siege of Bryant's Station

An Address.
By Reuben T. Durrett, Ll. D.,
President of the Filson Club.

The Lexington Chapter of the Daughters of the American Revolution have honoured me with the position of one of their speakers on this occasion. If any present, however, expect of me an attempt at oratory or display of eloquence, they will be disappointed. I am here in the interest of history, and it is my duty as well as my wish to deal plainly with facts only.

I shall confine what I have to say to the first act or stage in the siege of Bryant's Station on the 15th of August, 1782. It was during the first few hours of this siege that the women of the fort performed the heroic act which made them and the fort famous, and to these I propose to direct your attention on this occasion.

Object of the Meeting at Bryant's Station.

We have assembled here today for an extraordinary purpose. We propose to commemorate an heroic act performed by some of the pioneer women of Kentucky. The brave deeds of men, as they well deserved, have been celebrated in every age and clime. From the building of pyramids and the rearing of monoliths five thousand years ago until the present time the noble acts of brave men have been emblazoned on monumental stone.

When Pericles pronounced his funeral oration over the Athenians who had lost their lives in the battles of their country he said, "This whole world is the sepulchre of illustrious men." Women were not specifically included in this splendid eulogium of the great Grecian

Reuben T. Durrett, LL. D.,
President of the Filson Club

orator, and could not have been with truth. Exceptional gifts, like those of Sappho and Aspasia in the classic era, Heloise and Joan of Arc in the middle ages, and Madam Roland and Florence Nightingale in modern times, enabled their possessors to rise above the general oblivion of their sex and to receive from the world its monumental recognition. Such fortunate heroines have been few, however, and where one of their names has escaped the effacing fingers of time millions have been erased forever.

The world has never dealt justly with woman. Through ancient, through mediaeval, and down deep into modern times she has been rated and treated as an inferior being, as a creature put into this unequal world not for her own benefit but for the benefit of man. Her better day has at last dawned, and we now see her, where she should always have been, recognized in schools, colleges, and universities, in the learned professions, and in innumerable business pursuits, the avenues to which had been closed against her for thousands of years. This is but the beginning of the end. It is the glorious light of a brighter morning risen upon the noonday of human progress.

Our purpose here today is not to rear a stately monument to the memory of women whose fame fills the world, but to insure against oblivion the names of obscure heroines who helped to rescue Kentucky from the dominion of the savage.

The pioneer women who aided in laying the foundation of the Commonwealth of Kentucky are worthy of any honours we can pay them, and we propose to begin today with commemorative ceremonies in behalf of the wives and daughters who, at the risk of their own lives, enabled the garrison of Bryant's Station to escape the tomahawk and the scalping-knife of besieging savages by going out from the protecting walls of the fort and securing water from an exposed spring surrounded by the savage enemy.

We propose to dedicate to their memory a wall of enduring stone inclosing this spring and bearing their sacred names. These ceremonies, under the auspices of the Daughters of the American Revolution the act of women in behalf of women are peculiarly appropriate. If they should suggest the importance and justice of similar ceremonies in behalf of other pioneer women who sleep in unknown graves in different parts of our State, they will accomplish a good work beyond the immediate purpose of conferring honours on the heroines of Bryant's Station.

Before entering upon the specific act of the women which made

9

famous this spring and fort and hallowed the very ground[1] we now occupy, let us recall the old fort itself, and look upon it as it appeared in the day of its usefulness. All readers of Kentucky history are more or less familiar with the conventional pioneer forts in which our ancestors lived as a safeguard against the Indians, but the fort which stood here differed considerably from others and demands some particularity of description.

LOCATION OF BRYANT'S STATION.

It was beautifully located on the gradually sloping south bank of the head branch of the Elkhorn, in the midst of a dark forest of noble trees, here and there relieved by smiling canebrakes. From the summit of its northeastern block-house the waters of the Elkhorn could be partially seen between obstructing trees as the creek flowed in a crescent bend, near the centre of which on the south side was the bluff-hidden spring which supplied the inhabitants with water and above which stood the fort on a commanding elevation. From around it on all sides several hundred acres of the dense woods had been cleared away for the purpose of giving uninterrupted range to the rifles which defended it; but in full view, around the rim of the encircling forest yet uncut, stood great black walnut trees and blue ash trees and honey locust trees and sugar maple trees, seeming in their strength to boast of the soil that nourished them, while along the Elkhorn stood giant

---

1. Bryant's Station was situated about five miles from Lexington on the road leading to Paris. It stood near where this road crosses the Elkhorn Creek. The topography of the country, except in the absence of its once dense forest, differs but little from what it was when the station was besieged by the Indians one hundred and fourteen years ago. The land on which it stood, after remaining in the Rogers family for three generations, passed to Thomas Wood, who is the present owner. It is yet remarkable for a fertility which has survived more than a century of cultivation. It is literally in the heart of the bluegrass region of Kentucky, renowned for a soil as productive as the exuberant delta of the Nile. Our pioneers determined the rich land of the new country by the trees that grew upon it, and when they saw the fine walnuts and locusts and ashes and maples that grew here they knew the land was fertile and selected it.

2. In one of these grand old sycamores tradition has located an enterprising Indian during the siege. He had climbed high enough in the tree to look down into the fort and to pick off his white victims without being in danger himself while hidden by the foliage of the tree. The sound from his discharged rifle, however, directed the sharp eye of Jacob Stucker to his hiding-place, and the next moment he was on his way to the ground beneath with a deadly rifle ball through his body. The stump of the tree still stands on the bank of the Elkhorn, (as at time of first publication), and indicates in its decay its dimensions while living.

sycamores[2] like sentinels of old looking down upon the fortification they guarded. On the trace which led to Lexington on the southwest and to Limestone on the northeast was a field of more than one hundred acres of corn growing in the rank luxury which the rich soil from which it sprang imparted to it.

DUAL NAME OF THE STATION.

It was built in 1779 on ground which belonged to Colonel William Preston, of Virginia. In 1774 Colonel John Floyd surveyed a tract of one thousand acres here for Colonel Preston, who afterward exchanged it with Joseph Rogers for land in the Horseshoe Bottom on the New River. The fort was built principally by the Bryans of North Carolina, some of whom were in Kentucky as early as 1776, but who resided at Boonesborough and other stations until 1779. For some unknown reason it took the double name of Bryant and Bryan from the beginning, and was widely known by both names in early times. More than thirteen thousand acres of land in the neighbourhood of this station were entered in 1779 and 1780 by different members of the Bryan family, but none of them seems to have secured the land on which this station stood nor to have given it his distinctive name.

William Bryan, James Bryan, Morgan Bryan, Joseph Bryan, George Bryan, David Bryan, Samuel Bryan, and John Bryan each entered a portion of these lands more or less distant from the station, and, while the entries are in the name of Bryan, some of the lands are described as being such a distance or such a direction from Bryant's Station.[3] Cave Johnson, in his autobiography, states that he and William Tomlinson helped to erect this fort in 1779, and calls it Bryant's Station. The Commissioners, who were here in 1780 to adjust settlers' and improvers' rights to land under the law of 1779, called it Bryant[4] in the certificates they issued, and Colonel William Fleming, one of the Commissioners, entered it as Bryant in his journal. While, therefore, it must be conceded that persons by the distinctive name of Bryan were the principal builders and the most numerous and respectable

---

3. The records of our land office also show entries in 1780 and in subsequent years by persons of the distinctive name of Bryant Joseph Bryant, William Bryant, John Bryant, and James Bryant each entered lands in different parts of the State, and their entries, though not so large as those of the Bryans, amounted in the aggregate to nearly six thousand acres.

4. I have seen but one of these certificates which bore the name of Bryan, and that was not an original but a copy of the one issued to John South, December 25, 1779. All the others that I have seen gave the name of the station as Bryant's.

first inhabitants of the fort, there may have been others of the equally distinctive name of Bryant concerned sufficiently to affect the name. I continue to call it Bryant because I was first taught this name by our historians.

From Filson in 1784 to Collins in 1874, a period of ninety years, our historians uniformly call it Bryant's Station. The first of our historians to call it Bryan's was Richard H. Collins in 1874. Bryan would suit me equally well but for something of an antiquarian proclivity for primitive impressions. In fact, the names Bryant and Bryan seem to have been indiscriminately applied to this fort in early times, as if Bryan meant Bryant, and Bryant meant Bryan. It is therefore but a matter of choice or taste whether we of today shall retain or discard the final *t* in the spelling. "*De gustibus non est disputandum.*" See *Note* following.

> Note:—An example of this confused or indiscriminate use of the two names is supplied by the autobiography of Colonel Cave Johnson, a pioneer of more than average intelligence. While Johnson was on his way from Virginia to Kentucky, in 1779, he met on the Cumberland River some emigrants from North Carolina also on their way to Kentucky. There are reasons for believing that the right name of the persons thus met by Johnson was Bryan, and yet, after journeying with them to the Elkhorn and helping them to erect a station, Johnson calls them Bryant and the station they built Bryant's.
>
> The records of suits tried in our early Court of Appeals furnish other examples. In the case of George Bryan, &c., *v.* John Bradford, &c., Hughes' Kentucky *Reports*, and David Bryan, &c. , *v.* Caleb Wallace, the complainants, who are seeking title to lands in the neighbourhood of this very station, are called Bryan and the station itself Bryant.
>
> In the book of land entries kept by George May for the State there is an entry on the 20th of May, 1780, in the name of William Bryant, for one thousand nine hundred and thirty-two acres, and another entry of the same quantity of land on the 1st of August, 1783, in the name of William Bryan. In this second entry the original entry on the trace from Louisville to Bullitt's Lick is withdrawn and land near Chenowith's Run substituted, so that the same man must have first entered as Bryant in 1780 and as Bryan in 1783.

BRYANT'S STATION DRAWN BY MISS JEAN H. MCHENRY, FROM THE GROUND PLAN OF GENERAL GEORGE ROGERS CLARK.

Daniel Boone, in his letter to the Governor of Virginia, written soon after the siege of the station, calls it Bryan's, but soon after, when dictating his biography to John Filson, he calls it Briant's. And Filson himself, while calling it Briant in the text of his life of Boone in his *History of Kentucky*, published in 1784, on his map to accompany his history enters it Bryan's. In the midst of such a confusion of names by those who knew one another more than an hundred years ago, it is hardly to be expected that we of this late day can straighten out the tangle. We may properly enough follow the example of our ancestors and call the station Bryant's or Bryan's, as choice or occasion requires.

DESCRIPTION OF BRYANT'S STATION.

The fort was built in the form of a parallelogram six hundred feet long and one hundred and fifty feet wide. In this extreme length, compared with its breadth, was the principal difference between it and other forts. Most of the forts were parallelograms having a length of about one third in excess of their breadth. Many of them were as wide as Bryant's, but none of them so long. Its extreme length, possibly, came of the wish of the inhabitants to have as much open space between their cabins as possible. Placed at irregular intervals on both of the exterior long sides of this parallelogram were twenty log cabins, sixteen feet square and one story high, some with dirt and others with puncheon floors, but all with inward-sloping board roofs and wooden chimneys. The outer walls of the cabins, with pickets filling the spaces between them, formed the walls of the fort on each of the two long sides. There was a folding gate of heavy timber, eight feet wide, on each of the long sides.

There were no cabins on the narrow ends, but pickets only. The outer cabin walls and pickets were twelve feet high, and formed a good protection against anything but cannon. At each of the four corners was a strong block-house extending two feet further out than the other cabins and two stories high, with the upper story projecting two feet outside of the lower. This extension beyond the outer walls of the other cabins gave the garrison an enfilading fire at the enemy along the walls, while the projection of the upper story beyond the lower gave them a perpendicular fire at the enemy below. It was very unsafe for the enemy to attempt a lodgement near the fort walls or at the gates when these block-houses were properly manned.

These corner houses were generally occupied by the men of the fort who had no families, and were large enough to accommodate a goodly number of this important class of inhabitants. The cabins were generally occupied by families. There was a fine spring which poured a generous stream of clear, cool water from the southern bank of the Elkhorn, but it was not included within the walls.

It was, however, within range of the rifles of the fort, and thus erroneously considered safe. It was the act of the brave women of Bryant's Station in coming here for water, within range of hundreds of loaded rifles in the hands of concealed savages, that made this spring a leading object of commemoration today. Like the famous spring near Rome, which has for twenty-five centuries borne the name of the nymph whose fair form melted into its crystal waters and became a part of them, this spring, with its wall and its tablets of stone dedicated today, should preserve the name and the fame of those heroines who made it immortal.[5]

How They Lived in Bryant's Station.

The life lived in the cabins at Bryant's was not unlike that of other stations. There could be no such thing as luxury or even comfort there in the wilderness of Kentucky, five hundred miles distant from any other abode of civilization. The rich and the poor lived almost alike,

---

5. When Bryant's Station was besieged there were, perhaps, as many as sixty other similar stations scattered over the State. Some of them, however, consisted of only a few contiguous cabins, and were hardly worthy of the name. The fort at Boonesborough, the first built, and a kind of model for all others, was about two hundred feet long and one hundred and twenty feet wide, and consisted of thirty cabins, including the block-houses at the four corners. Harrodsburg, Lexington, and Stanford had forts that differed but little in size and cabin capacity from that at Boonesborough. Linn's and Floyd's and Sullivan's and the Dutch and Spring stations on Beargrass occupied a little more ground, but did not materially differ from the Boonesborough model. Fort Nelson, at Louisville, was the next largest in the State after Bryant's. It was two hundred and ten feet square, and was surrounded by a ditch and wall as well as by pickets. It was built to resist cannon, and was the only fort in the State that could stand a bombardment. It was never assailed by cannon, although Bird intended to try it in 1780, but changed his mind. He attacked Ruddle's and Martin's stations on the Licking instead, and made them surrender to his two field-pieces without any damaging shots. None of the forts had the springs which supplied them with water inclosed within the walls except Spring Station on Beargrass and the Lexington Station, and none of them except Bryant's had all the cabins covered with shed roofs that sloped inward. It was this form of roof which saved Bryant's from being consumed by the lighted Indian arrows fired upon them at the siege. The boys who were raised to the roofs to extinguish the fire would have been picked off by the Indians except for this form of roof which protected them.

for the simple reason that there was but little for those with money to buy which was not equally enjoyed by those without money. The cabins contained furniture of the rudest kind, which could be made with the axe, the saw, and the auger. The bedstead was made by inserting forks in the floor and running poles through the prongs to bear boards on which the bedding lay. A buffalo robe formed the mattress, while bear skins and deer skins supplied the covering. The dining-table was a puncheon hewed smooth with the broadaxe and supported by four sticks set into as many auger holes at the corners. The chairs were three-legged stools without backs. The cupboard consisted of boards laid on pegs driven in the corner wall.

The table furniture was made up of wooden plates, bowls, and trenchers, usually turned from the buck-eye. There were a few pewter plates and spoons, and delft cups and saucers, and two-pronged iron forks, and case- knives, and tin cups which had been brought from the old settlements, but they were not in general use. It required an itinerant preacher or a distinguished stranger to bring such finery to the table. The fireplace occupied nearly one whole side of the cabin; the window, where the light entered through greased paper, was a hole left by sawing out a few feet of one of the logs, and the door was simply a larger opening made by sawing out parts of more logs and covering the aperture with a buffalo skin.

Near the door two prongs of a buck's horn were fastened to the wall and on them suspended the long-barrelled, flint-lock rifle, without which no cabin was considered furnished. After the clothes with which they came from the mother country were reduced to rags that could no longer be patched, the men wore buckskin breeches, hunting-shirts, and *moccasins*, with raccoon or fox skin caps; and the women, such coarse linsey gowns as they could make by spinning on the little wheel and weaving on the hand loom the lint of the wild nettle and the wool of the buffalo. The buffalo, the deer, the bear, and the wild turkey furnished the principal meat, while Indian corn supplied the usual bread.[6]

The constant struggle for something to eat and to wear and the ceaseless danger from the Indians left but little time for amusement, and yet the men had foot races and horse races and shooting matches,

---

6. When corn was scarce the breast of the wild turkey was considered an excellent substitute for bread. Especially was this the case after the hard winter of 1779-1780, when the little corn that had been raised the previous season was consumed by the large number of immigrants who came into the country.

while the women enjoyed quiltings and knittings and maple sugar makings. Of rainy days and nights the young, and sometimes the old also, assembled in one of the block-houses to hear the merry sounds of the fiddle, in the hands of some old Virginia negro, and to dance away loneliness and sorrow and care.[7]

We have now had something of a view of Bryant's Station as it existed when besieged by the Indians, and let us next consider the movements of the enemy which made the bringing of water into it so dangerous and so necessary.

Origin of the Attack on Bryant's Station.

In the spring of 1782 Captain William Caldwell,[8] a British officer in Canada, collected a large body of Indians for the purpose of attacking Wheeling, Virginia. While on his way to Wheeling, runners from the Shawnees informed him that General George Rogers Clark was marching an army of Kentuckians against their towns. Caldwell at once abandoned his expedition and counter-marched to Chillicothe and Piqua for the protection of the Indian towns where Xenia and Springfield, in Ohio, now stand. He had a large army consisting of eleven hundred Indians collected, and three hundred more within supporting distance, and was anxious to be attacked by the Kentuckians; but the information he had received turned out to be false.

Some of the Shawnee spies had seen the gunboat which General Clark had invented to patrol the Ohio River land men at the mouth of the Licking, and had concluded that Clark was collecting an army

---

7. Fighting may also be listed among the pastimes without seriously violating the truth. It was certainly deemed a kind of amusement for two men to engage in a rough and tumble contest and for others to look on and enjoy the skill, strength, and endurance displayed. So long as the combatants confined themselves to blows with the hands and kicks with the feet no particular harm was done; but now and then they would bite and gouge, and the result was not unfrequently an ear or nose bitten off or an eyeball dislodged from its socket. If one called another a liar, the one so denounced must resent the insult by a fight. He might be worsted in the encounter, but could hardly come off with less injury than would be his lot if he did not resent the insult and save himself from the name of coward.

8. Caldwell was an Irishman by birth who lived in Pennsylvania at the commencement of the Revolution. Contrary to what might be expected from his nationality, he became a loyalist and fought against the Colonies. He went to Detroit and became efficient with McKee and Girty and Gibson and others in leading the savages against Kentucky, Virginia, etc. The company he kept shows him to have been about upon a par with the rest of the renegade scoundrels who forgot their white blood and became enamoured of the red stream of Indian barbarity.

there to invade their country. This false news disgusted both Caldwell and his Indians, and the greater part of his savage allies deserted him. He had a considerable force left, however, among whom were three hundred Wyandot and Lake Indians. These Wyandots were the warriors who, man to man, defeated Captain Estill's company in March, 1782, and were justly regarded as the best fighting men of all the Indian tribes. With this force he resolved to march against Bryant's Station in Kentucky, rather than return home without a victory or even an engagement. He was ashamed to return home without a fight.[9]

— This Alexander McKee was a notorious renegade, who went hand in hand with the Girtys in conducting Indian raids into Kentucky. Previous to the Revolution he was a loyal white citizen of Pennsylvania, and acquired two thousand acres of land on the south branch of the Elkhorn, in Kentucky, for services in the French and Indian wars. In 1778 he deserted the cause of the Colonies, and with Girty and Gibson went among the Indians to help them to scalp and tomahawk his own former countrymen. His lands on the Elkhorn were confiscated in 1780, and became the property of Transylvania University. Kentuckians are indebted to his fiendish intellect and cruel heart for the murder of many innocent women and children, who but for his ability and ferocity might have escaped. He no doubt enjoyed the slaughter of Kentuckians at the Battle of the Blue Licks, which occurred so near to the lands that had been escheated from him. He was a savage in everything except birth and colour, and, unfortunately for humanity, had a head with brains enough in it to make him more to be dreaded than even the Girtys.

The Renegade Simon Girty.

It is probable that when the disappointed Indians were returning to their towns, and Caldwell was doing all he could to retain enough of them for an expedition to Kentucky, the infamous Simon Girty attempted to inspire them by his celebrated speech. Girty was a white man by birth, but had been so long among the Indians that he was as much a savage as the worst of them. He seems to have cultivated a fierce hatred of his own race for the purpose of making himself the more acceptable to the Indians. While he had considerable influence

---

9. Official letter of Captain William Caldwell to Commander A. S. DePeyster, at Detroit, giving his account of the siege of Bryant's Station and the Battle of the Blue Licks. Haldeman Manuscripts, in Canadian Archives, Series B, Volume 123. Also official letter of Captain Alexander McKee.

over his savage allies, he does not seem to have risen to the command of them in any very important military expedition.

The most important office he ever held was that of Indian interpreter, and he sometimes disgraced this position by false and malicious translations. Kentucky historians have made him the commander-in-chief in the siege of Bryant's Station and the Battle of the Blue Licks, but later information, not accessible when they wrote, shows this to have been a mistake. Captain Caldwell was the first in command, and Girty, though prominent and efficient, occupied a secondary position. Girty 's speech at Chillicothe to inflame the Indians against the Kentuckians, and his plea for a surrender during the siege of Bryant's Station, were parts of the important but dirty and subordinate work assigned him by his superiors. The following is his speech at Chillicothe, as given in Bradford's *Notes* on Kentucky:

GIRTY'S SPEECH TO THE INDIANS.

Brothers: The fertile region of Kentucky is the land of cane and clover, spontaneously growing to feed the buffalo, the elk, and the deer; there the bear and the beaver are always fat. The Indians from all the tribes have had a right, from time immemorial, to hunt and kill, unmolested, these wild animals and bring off their skins to purchase for themselves clothing, to buy blankets for their backs and rum to send down their throats to drive away the cold and rejoice their hearts after the fatigue of hunting and the toil of war. [Great applause from the crowd.]

But, brothers, the Long Knives have overrun your country and usurped your hunting-ground; they have destroyed the cane, trodden down the clover, killed the deer and the buffalo, the bear and the raccoon. The beaver has been chased from his dam and forced to leave the country. [Palpable emotion among the hearers.]

Brothers, the intruders on your lands exult in the success that has crowned their flagitious act. They are planting fruit trees and ploughing the lands, where not long since were the canebrake and the clover field. Was there a voice in the trees of the forest, or articulate sounds in the gurgling waters, every part of this country would call on you to chase away these ruthless invaders who are laying it waste. Unless you rise in the majesty of your might and extermine their whole race, you may bid *adieu* to the hunting-grounds of your fathers, to the delicious flesh of the animals with which it once abounded, and to the skins with which you were once enabled to purchase your clothing and your rum."[10]

NUMBER OF INDIANS WHO ATTACKED BRYANT'S STATION.

Bradford, unlike Humphrey Marshall and other historians, has given this speech in the first person, as delivered, with the plaudits of the hearers to indicate the impression it made. We cannot say that he may not have had a manuscript copy in that form, since we know that the celebrated speech of Logan to the whites at Camp Charlotte, and that of Bullitt to the Indians at Chillicothe, have come down to us in the first person. Not long after Girty's harangue was finished the march for Kentucky began. How many Indians were in the expedition can never be known with any degree of certainty. Captain Caldwell, their commander, says in his official report that he had three hundred Wyandots, Lake Indians, and Rangers.

Alexander McKee, who also made an official report to the Canadian authorities, adds some Delawares and Shawnees to those mentioned by Caldwell, and thus swells the number beyond three hundred. Bradford, in his Notes on Kentucky, makes the Indians five hundred and sixty, and the Canadians and Tories sixty, or a total of six hundred and twenty; Colonel Boone estimates them at from four hundred to five hundred, and our historians who give numbers generally mention from five hundred to six hundred as the strength of the invading army. It is possible that a mean of some four hundred, between the two extremes, will be nearer the truth.

DATE OF THE ATTACK ON BRYANT'S STATION.

There is also conflicting authority as to the date at which the Indian army reached Bryant's Station. Colonel Daniel Boone, Colonel Levi Todd, and Colonel Benjamin Logan, neither of whom was at the

---

10. If this speech was not vouched for as here given by John Bradford in his *Notes on Kentucky*, and substantially by Humphrey Marshall in his *History of Kentucky*, I should entertain grave doubts as to its authenticity. It is, to say the least of it, a pretty high order of speech for such an unlettered miscreant as Girty to make. Of course it was not delivered in the English language, as here given, but in the Indian tongue, and then translated. We know that there were some Kentuckians taken two years before, at Ruddle's and Martin's stations, prisoners, with the Indians when the speech was made, and it is possible that one of them might have secured and sent or brought home a copy. In behalf of the Indians it would have been difficult for any orator to have made a more effective speech, but coming from a white man it was the speech of a monster of iniquity monstrously uttered.

fort when the siege began, but the first-named two of whom were in the Battle of the Blue Licks which followed, in their letters to the Governor of Virginia, published in the Virginia Calendar, agree as to the date of attack having been August the 16th. On the contrary, Captain Caldwell, who commanded the expedition, and ought to have known the exact date as well as anyone else, in his official report, already alluded to, gives the 15th of August as the date.

All Kentucky historians, from Filson, in 1784, to Smith, in 1892, as well as journals and letters of private citizens written at the time, agree with commanding officer Caldwell that the 15th of August was the day on which the siege began. There is authority therefore for different dates, and I have adhered to the 15th of August, 1782, because I have been made used to this date by our historians, and have not yet seen sufficient reasons for changing a date thus permanently fixed in our history.[11]

PLAN OF THE ATTACK ON THE STATION.

When Bryant's Station was reached before daylight on the morning of August 15, 1782, it was immediately surrounded by the Indians. Caldwell's plan seems to have been to place a detachment of Indians in full view on the southeast side of the fort, where the road led to Lexington and to Limestone, while the main body were concealed on the northwest side near the spring from which the fort was supplied with water. At daylight the exposed detachment were to fire on the fort and make such noisy demonstrations as would draw out the garrison to engage them. When this should be done, the main body on the opposite side were to rush upon the fort, break down its gate, and carry it by storm.

COUNTER PLAN OF THE DEFENDERS OF THE STATION.

This plan of Caldwell would have been excellent, provided there had been no one in the fort capable of interpreting it so soon as it

---

11. Three of our earliest historians, John Filson, Humphrey Marshall, and John Bradford, were in Kentucky when the Indians besieged Bryant's Station. They were men of superior intelligence, and as likely to know as well as anyone else when such important events as the siege of Bryant's Station occurred. Each of them gives the 15th of August, 1782, as the date of the siege. They must be regarded as contemporary historians of the event, and for this reason entitled to the fullest credit. Another contemporary writer was Colonel Andrew Steel, who, in his letter to the Governor of Virginia, dated August the 26th, 1782, says the siege began on the 15th of August, 1782.

21

began to be executed. The garrison had been preparing the previous night to march at daylight to the relief of Hoy's Station,[12] and, as the gates were opened in the morning for the exit of the men, the decoy party of Indians began firing and inviting an engagement by their boisterous demonstrations. The gates were immediately closed and the action of the Indians subjected to scrutiny. Their conduct was so contrary to their usual secret mode of attack that it was at once interpreted as a ruse. Caldwell's plan of attack was as plainly read by those in command of the fort as if it had been written out and diagrammed before them. They determined at once that this boisterous display of a small party of Indians in full view of one side of the fort meant that the main body was concealed on the other side, and would assault the fort so soon as it should be emptied of men by an engagement with the decoy detachment.

The Indian plan of attack had therefore to be counteracted, and this was done with the prompt decision peculiar to the pioneers. It was determined to repair any defects that might exist in the fort on the northwest side, and to station there all available men with loaded guns ready for a concentrated discharge. When this should be done, a party of men were to be sent out on the opposite side of the fort to pursue the decoy Indians a short distance, and help them to as much noise and firing as possible, so as to make the main body of the Indians concealed on the northwest side think that the garrison was really engaged with the decoy party, as they themselves had planned, and the fort consequently left inhabited by only women and children.

The Want of Water in the Station

All things having been arranged in accordance with this plan, and the men and boys large enough to handle rifles stationed with loaded guns on the northwest side, there was one more important want to be provided for. There was no water in the fort, and the burning August sun would soon be sending down his perpendicular rays upon the be-

---

12. Hoy's Station was in Madison County, on the site of the present village of Foxtown. The Indians had defeated Captain Holder on the 14th in an engagement at the Upper Blue Licks, and it had been determined to assemble all available help at Hoy's for its protection, and for another engagement with the Indians. It is possible that this was just what Caldwell wanted. He may have aimed at this result for the purpose of the more easily taking Bryant's Station when part of its garrison had gone to Hoy's. If such was his plan, he came very near accomplishing it, and would have been fully successful if those about to march from Bryant's to Hoy's had had a little more time to make their start.

leaguered garrison. The thought of successfully resisting a siege without water was out of the question. The tongues of the men swollen by dry heat would fill their mouths and render them speechless, while the burning brain would succumb to the fatal torpor of sunstroke. However abundant might be guns and ammunition, their use in the only way that they could be beneficial would be hurtful from the fact that the gas from the burnt powder would help the blazing sun to increase the deadly thirst. Death by the *tomahawk* and scalping-knife could not have been more certain than by the delirium and coma of a burning brain.

How to obtain the necessary water was a serious question. The spring[13] from which it was to be brought was near where the main body of the Indians were concealed. Hundreds of rifles in the hands of bloodthirsty savages were in point-blank range of the only source of the indispensable water. How was the water to be obtained without the risk of life? The Craigs, who were the principal men in the fort, solved this question with the same wisdom with which they had interpreted the plan of Caldwell. They assumed that the Indians were in ambush at the spring and that they would not unmask until their decoy party on the other side of the fort gave evidence of being engaged with the garrison.

If, however, the women of the fort, as was their habit, should go to the spring for water, it was believed that the Indians would not interfere with them—that they would not, for the sake of capturing a few women, risk the loss of the whole fort which they expected to take by remaining concealed until the proper time. It was believed, moreover, that Captain Caldwell, having formed his plan, would have neither time nor opportunity for changing it for the purpose of capturing the women.

THE FEMALES OF THE STATION GO TO THE SPRING FOR WATER.

---

13. This spring was on the southern bank of the Elkhorn, a little to the westward of a line drawn northward from the westerly fort gate to the creek and about sixty yards from the northerly end of the fort. The creek bank or bluff that rose above it and from which it issued concealed it from view at the fort, and it was surrounded by trees and shrubs and cane and weeds which afforded ample hiding-places for the Indians. From their concealment near the spring they could move among the trees and undergrowth along the creek into the cornfield on the other side of the fort almost without danger or exposure. This does not speak very well for the military genius which planned the fort, especially as concealed enemies so near it could have been avoided by simply clearing away the growth about the spring and along the creek.

The women of the fort were therefore brought together and the situation explained to them. Even if some of them may have thought that it would have been braver and at least more gallant for the men to go to the spring for water, there were leaders among them who promptly took the same view of the situation that the men had presented.

Tradition has handed down the name of Jemima Suggett Johnson, the wife of Colonel Robert Johnson, as the heroine who first spoke approval and led the way to the spring. Her husband was far away at the capital of Virginia, and she had an infant son in the cradle and two little boys and two little girls with her in the fort.

She hesitated not, however, to leave her infant child to the care of his little sister Sally and his little brothers James and William, while she took Betsy, aged ten, to help bring water, and marched with the bold water-bearers to the spring. Under her lead all moved with firm step and fearless eye along the path that led from the northwestern gate to the spring, like Amazons of old following their Queen Myrena from the seclusion of the Island of Hesperia to the open field of danger.

When they had reached the spring and filled their pails and piggins and noggins with water and returned to the fort without having been disturbed by the Indians, the wisdom of the whites in divining the plan of attack had been vindicated.

But what a mistake the Indians made in their own interest in not seizing the women at the spring and holding them as prisoners! With these wives and mothers and daughters in their possession they might have compelled a surrender of the fort which their arms could not accomplish.

THE ATTACK AND REPULSE OF THE INDIANS.

When the women, with their vessels filled with water, re-entered the fort and the northwest gate had been closed behind them, the southeast gate was opened and a dozen or more young men went out to make a mock attack upon the decoy party of Indians. The rapid firing and the tumultuous noise made by these deceptive assailants and assailed—for both were instructed to make all the noise they could—induced the main body of Indians on the northwest side to believe that the whole garrison were warmly engaged with their decoy party, as they themselves had designed, and that the undefended fort was at their mercy.

They rushed out from their ambuscade and, like famished tigers in sight of blood, sprang upon the fort; but to their surprise found it manned at every point on the side of attack.[14] A deadly shower of rifle balls was poured into their dense ranks, dealing wounds and death in every direction, and compelling them to retreat without having done much damage beyond having set fire to some of the cabins. They set fire to some out-buildings near the fort, which might have proved serious except for an easterly wind which blew the flames from the fort. The flames that had been kindled within the fort walls were speedily extinguished by the children who were lifted to the burning roofs by their mothers and handed water for the purpose.

It is known that James Johnson, a boy of eight, was lifted to a cabin roof fired by a lighted arrow and given a piggin of water to pour on the fire by his mother, and it is reasonable to assume that the mothers of the Craig, the Saunders, and the Cave children did likewise with their boys, who were too little to handle guns, but too big to be idle in such an emergency. And, as if to add a brighter glow to the halo which already encircled the brows of the water-bearing females of the fort, a lighted arrow from an Indian bow fell upon the sugar-trough cradle in which the infant, Richard M. Johnson, was lying. His little sister Betsy promptly extinguished the flame, and thus saved from certain injury and possible death him who afterward became the hero of the Battle of the Thames, and rose to the vice-presidency of the United States.

The first assault on Bryant's Station had thus proved a failure, and the prospect of increased strength in the garrison from neighbouring forts which had been applied to for help was ominous of even worse results should another attack be made. A victory so far as the fort was concerned was practically won by the garrison, and was so considered by the besieging and the besieged. Indians are not the kind of soldiers to make a second assault upon a fortified place when a first attempt

14. When the siege began there were forty-four men in the fort, as stated by Bradford in his *Notes on Kentucky* (MSS.), Section 13; but two of them, Nicholas Tomlinson and Thomas Bell, were sent out to procure help from other stations, so that the force was reduced to forty-two. To this number, however, must be added the boys in the fort big enough to handle rifles, who probably swelled the defensive force to fifty or more. After the siege had progressed for several hours a party of sixteen mounted men made their way into the station; but we are at present concerned only with the defenders who were in the fort when the siege began.

15. Quite a number of Indians were killed during the siege, but how many we shall never know. Caldwell, in his report to the Canadian authorities, before cited, only admits five killed and two wounded. This small number is not reasonable, however, when the concentrated fire of the garrison at short range into the thick ranks of the assailants is considered. (Continued next page).

has been a bloody failure.[15]

Let us at this point drop the narrative of the siege and make such a record as we can of the names of the men, women, and children who were in the fort when it was besieged. Especially is such a record due to the heroic women and girls who were there, but whom our historians up to this time have failed to mention by name. The heroic men who resisted the siege have been mentioned by name and by deed, as they should have been, but the women have been neglected. Jemima Suggett Johnson was incidentally mentioned in the Centenary Address on the one hundredth anniversary of the birth of Kentucky, published by the Filson Club in 1892, but with this single exception history has been silent as to the names of these heroines who performed an act which for cool and deliberate courage has never been surpassed.

INHABITANTS OF THE STATION WHEN THE SIEGE BEGAN.

There were but few families in the station when the siege began. None of the Bryans, who at first formed its most numerous and efficient inhabitants, was there. They had been so discouraged by the capture of Martin's and Ruddle's stations, by the breaking up of the station of their relative, Grant, by the death of John Bryan and the killing of William Bryan[16] by the Indians in 1780, that they had all returned with their families to their old homes in North Carolina in August, 1780, and did not come back until 1784.[17] Neither Colonel Robert Johnson nor his brother, Cave Johnson, was there. Colonel Johnson had been elected to the Virginia Legislature that year, and he and his brother Cave were

---

Colonel Boone says thirty Indians were killed. In the fort, Robert Adkinson and David Mitchell were killed, and Nicholas Tomlinson wounded. Tomlinson recovered from his wounds and was afterward killed in Harmer's expedition in 1790. He was in the advance of the detachment of Colonel John Hardin when he was riddled with bullets by Indians in ambuscade. (Bradford's *Notes on Kentucky*, MSS.)

16. There were two William Bryans who figured in the early records of Kentucky— William Bryan, senior, and William Bryan, junior. The records of our land office show land entries in both of these names. Our historians, however, have not sufficiently drawn the distinction between them to enable us to distinguish whether it was the senior or the junior Bryan who was killed in 1780, while leading out a hunting party to procure meat for the station. Colonel William Fleming in his journal (MSS.) states that William Bryant, junior, was killed on the 10th of March, 1780, about four miles from the station. He uses the name Bryant, but as no one named William Bryant is known to have been killed at that date, and as one named William Bryan is known to have been killed about this time, he must mean William Bryan, junior.

17. David Bryan, &c., *v.* Caleb Wallace, Hughes' *Kentucky Reports*.

in Virginia at the time. Had it not been for the coming of the Johnsons and the Craigs and others under their influence after the departure of the Bryans, the fort would have been abandoned.

At the siege it had but twelve families to occupy its forty cabins, and was principally garrisoned by men whose services were in demand as hunters, land locators, surveyors, and Indian scouts and spies. We may never know all who were in the fort at the time, but the subjoined list, made up from history, from court records, from land entries, from official surveys, from manuscript journals, from unpublished letters, from old newspapers, and from tradition, though not claimed to be perfect, may suffice to rescue from the neglect of one hundred and fourteen years some names too precious to sink permanently into undeserved oblivion. In the difficult task of making up this list, it is due to Miss Lucretia H. Clay, of Lexington, to Mrs. John C. Sherley, of Anchorage, to Colonel J. Stoddard Johnston, of Louisville, and to the pioneer, Doctor Stephen F. Gano, of Scott County, that I should here acknowledge my indebtedness for valuable aid and confirmatory information.

It has been generally accepted as true that Elijah Craig was in command of the fort when the siege began. That the Craigs were the principal men in the fort at the time there can be no doubt, but there is good ground for want of faith as to the fort having been under the command of Elijah Craig. There were two Elijah Craigs prominent in pioneer times in Kentucky, one the Reverend Elijah, a Baptist preacher of great intellect and character, and Captain Elijah, his nephew, also possessed of rare endowments; but as the Reverend Elijah did not settle in Kentucky until after the siege of Bryant's Station, he could not have been in command. Captain John Craig, the father, and Captain Jeremiah Craig, the uncle of Captain Elijah, both men of considerable military reputation, were in the fort at the time, and it is more likely that one of them was in command. In a list of the children of Taliafero Craig, senior, embracing all the Craigs who came to Kentucky, by Albert G. Craig, of Vevay, Indiana, it is stated that Captain John Craig commanded the fort when it was besieged, and such is my belief.

Some of those named in the list here given are known to have been

---

18. Some of the men have been mentioned by our historians, but none of the women and children. Marshall, edition of 1812, page 161, and edition of 1824, volume 1, mentions some of them; Bradford (MSS.), Section 13, others, and Collins, volume 2, others. Collins also mentions others in an article on the Battle of the Blue Licks, published in the *Courier-Journal* August 19, 1882. (Continued next page).

in the fort, and it is believed that most if not all of them were there.[18]

LIST OF PERSONS IN THE FORT WHEN THE SIEGE BEGAN.

Jemima Suggett Johnson and her children, Betsy, James, William, Sally, and Richard M.

Captain John Craig, his wife Sara Page, and their children, John H., Betsy, Elijah, Sally, Benjamin, Lewis, Nancy, Philip, Frank, and Polly.

Captain Jeremiah Craig, his wife Lucy Hawkins, and their children, Elijah, Polly, Frankey, and Hawkins.

Toliver Craig, senior, his wife Polly Hawkins, and their daughter Sally.

Toliver Craig, junior, his wife Elizabeth Johnson, and their children, John, William, Nathaniel, Toliver, Elijah, Polly, and Nancy.

John Saunders, his wife Jane Craig, and their children, Polly, Betsy, Lydia, Nathaniel, and John.

Richard Cave, his wife Elizabeth Craig, and their children, Reuben, Hannah, and Polly.

Ranck, in his *History of Lexington*, and McBride, in his *Pioneer Biography*, volume 1, add others. Subsequent historians and biographers add no new names but simply repeat those given by their predecessors. A manuscript genealogy of the Craig family, prepared by Mrs. John C. Sherley, a great-granddaughter of the Reverend Elijah Craig, gives all the names of the Craigs as well as those of the Caves and Saunderses; and a similar work, prepared for the Johnson family by the Honourable Thomas L. Johnson, supplies the names of all the Johnsons. The records of land entries kept by George May in Kentucky while it was a part of Virginia show the names of nearly all of the men mentioned in this list who had secured farms in Kentucky before the siege of Bryant's. Some of these entries were of large bodies of land, and especially those of Captain John Craig, which aggregated over 20,000 acres. Doctor Coleman Rogers, a distinguished Louisville physician in early times, stated to the author that his father, Joseph Rogers, and his uncle, Barnett Rogers, were both in the fort; and Doctor C. C. Graham, another distinguished physician, who lived beyond an hundred years, made a similar statement as to his father, James Graham.

Both Doctor Graham and Doctor Rogers had recollections of nearly everyone in the fort which they had heard from their parents and from others. The Herndons of Henry County preserved family traditions of those of their name in the fort, and so did the Mitchells of the same county as to their ancestors. Doctor Lyman Beecher Todd, in a letter to the author, mentions John Suggett and his wife and child; the Honourable French Tipton, in a letter to the author, names Edward Nelson and wife; William D. Hixson also, in a letter to the author, adds Wainright Lea and wife and John Hammond and wife; and Jennie M. Hudelson also, in a letter to the author, gives the names of Thomas Ficklin and his wife and two children. Combining all these scattered authorities together they embrace nearly every name in this list of persons in the fort when the siege began.

Thomas Ficklin, his wife Mary Herndon, and their children, Joseph and Philadelphia.

John Suggett, his wife Mildred Davis, and their child William.

Wainright Lea and his wife, Fanny Sanders Lea.

John Hammond and his wife, Sarah Clement Hammond.

Edward Nelson and his wife, Harriet Morgan Nelson.

Aaron Reynolds, Thomas Bell, Jacob Stucker, Nicholas Tomlinson, William Tomlinson, Richard Mitchell, David Mitchell, William Mitchell, Dudley Mitchell, Thomas Herndon, Samuel Herndon, Edward Herndon, Zachariah Herndon, Robert Adkinson, James Graham, Daniel Wilcoxen, Martin Hammond, Ezekiel Field, William Field, Elison Williams, Barnett Rogers, Joseph Rogers, Jesse Yocum, Whitfield Craig, William Ledgerwood, James Ledgerwood, James Mitchum, John Mitchum, and James McBride. [19]

From this list of men, women, and children, ninety in number, it is not difficult to select the names of the females who went to the spring for water and became the heroines of the occasion. They were women and girls, mothers and children, wives and daughters. All of the boys in the fort who were old enough acted as men in firing rifles at the besieging Indians, and all of the girls who were old enough helped the women to bring water from the spring. The little girls could not, like their mothers, carry a pail of water in each hand, but they could manage one pail, or piggin, and thus two of them might equal one grown woman. It must be said, however, that some of the women carried a pail on the head and a pail in each hand, so that it would require three girls to equal one of them.

Here, then, is the final roll of honour, made up of the mothers who went to the spring and their daughters who were old enough to help them bring water:

LIST OF WOMEN & GIRLS WHO WENT TO THE SPRING FOR WATER.

Mrs. Jemima Suggett Johnson, wife of Colonel Robert John-

19. I have not included in this list James Morgan and his wife and child, who were in one of the cabins outside of the fort when the siege began. Morgan escaped with his child to Lexington, and his wife was taken prisoner by the Indians, so that neither of them got into the fort. They met after the Battle of the Blue Licks, and became the hero and heroine of one of the most thrilling adventures in pioneer times. Morgan, believing his wife had been consumed in their cabin, had laid himself down to die of wounds received in the Battle of the Blue Licks, when she, after escaping from her Indian captors, came upon him and saved his life.

son, and her daughter, Betsy Johnson.

Mrs. Sara Page Craig, wife of Captain John Craig, and her daughters, Betsy Craig, Sally Craig, Nancy Craig, and Polly Craig.

Mrs. Lucy Hawkins Craig, wife of Captain Jeremiah Craig, and her daughters, Polly Craig and Frankey Craig.

Mrs. Polly Hawkins Craig, wife of Toliver Craig, senior, and her daughter, Sally Craig.

Mrs. Elizabeth Johnson Craig, wife of Toliver Craig, junior, and her daughters, Polly Craig and Nancy Craig.

Mrs. Jane Craig Saunders, wife of John Saunders, and her daughters, Polly Saunders, Betsy Saunders, and Lydia Saunders.

Mrs. Elizabeth Craig Cave, wife of Richard Cave, and her daughters, Hannah Cave and Polly Cave.

Mrs. Fanny Sanders Lea, wife of Wainright Lea.

Mrs. Sara Clement Hammond, wife of John Hammond.

Mrs. Harriet Morgan Nelson, wife of Edward Nelson.

Mrs. Mary Herndon Ficklin, wife of Thomas Ficklin, and her daughter, Philadelphia Ficklin.

Mrs. Mildred Davis Suggett, wife of John Suggett.

THE ACT OF THE FEMALES OF BRYANT'S CONTRASTED WITH OTHER BRAVE DEEDS.

It thus appears that there were twelve grown women and sixteen misses who performed the perilous act of supplying the fort with water. Their act has scarcely a parallel in history. The aquatores, whose duty it was to supply armies with water, encountered great dangers, but they were professionals paid for their services, while these women and girls were volunteers with no hope or desire of reward. Captain Thomas Speed, in a beautiful address to the alumnae of the Female High School, of Louisville, compared the act of the women of Bryant's Station to the daring deed of King David's three mighty men who broke through the ranks of the Philistines to secure water from the well of Bethlehem for their King. Their act was similar to that of the females of Bryant's Station in the object sought and in the risk of life to obtain it, but there the parallel ceases.

The mighty men of David were professional warriors who had before them the reward of a great king if they succeeded and an immortal record in the sacred annals of their country if they failed. And, indeed, the names of these ancient heroes, Adino, Eleazor, and Shammah, were recorded by Samuel, as they should have been, and have come down to our times. But who has seen a record of the names of the heroines of Bryant's Station? In our histories you will look in vain for one of them. The heroes, Thomas Bell, Nicholas Tomlinson, Aaron Reynolds, and others, have had their names and deeds proclaimed to the world, as they should have been, but all is silence as to these heroines. Alas! they were but women, and we are left to infer that our historians did not deem them worthy of an immortal place in their undying works. We of today think differently, and have begun the good work of rescuing each of their names from undeserved oblivion.[20]

The Lexington Chapter of the Daughters of the American Revolution are to be commended for the good work they have done today. They have not only builded a monument upon ground hallowed by sacred memories of the pioneer period of Kentucky, but have associated their memorial work with an act of their own sex which ranks with the noblest deeds ever performed by mortals. Trained soldiers

---

20. McClung, in his *Sketches of Western Adventure*, after a wonderfully graphic and thrilling description of the siege, indulges in a light vein as to the quick steps of the women to reach the fort gate when they returned from the spring. There was, however, nothing amusing in their act from beginning to end. All was too solemn for anything like humour. We can imagine the appearance of the procession of women and girls as they came out from the fort gate and made their way along the footpath beginning at the gate and zigzagging down to the spring. They had to walk in single file because the path was not wide enough for two to walk abreast. When they reached the spring their natural inclination was to do their work as quickly as possible and return to the protecting walls of the fort. But here a difficulty presented itself which they had not probably noticed before. The basin of the spring was not deep enough to plunge the vessels and thus fill them at once. They had to dip the water with gourds, and thus tediously and slowly fill their vessels. During this slow process, which lengthened moments into hours, a glance to the right or left might have met the glittering black eyes of bloodthirsty savages peeping from behind trees or from among the undergrowth which concealed them. Soldiers are trained to face such dangers, but for women and girls, unused to such things, the determination to defy the danger must have been great. Caldwell had fortunately so impressed upon his savage allies the necessity of remaining concealed until guns were heard on the other side of the fort that they moved not while the women walked from the fort to the spring and filled their vessels with water and then walked back to the fort. The women might have consoled themselves with the assurance that if it was hard for them to thus appear in the presence of concealed savages, it was yet harder for these savages to restrain their impulse to seize and scalp them. The girls were not probably fully aware of the danger incurred, but the women comprehended the situation fully, and by an act of cool and deliberate courage won for themselves a name which should never pass from the memorial page of our history.

and private citizens accustomed to danger have performed daring deeds in every age and country, but this was the act of women used to the peaceful fireside. Had men to whose guidance they were used gone out from the protecting walls of the fort with them their case might have been less trying, but they went alone, and their act stands in our history alone.

OTHER HEROINES AND PLACES WORTHY OF MONUMENTS.

It is to be hoped that the work begun today on this consecrated spot may continue until a public sentiment is created in the State which will cause suitable monuments to be reared to the memory of other heroines who now sleep in unknown graves. Kentucky's unwritten history is full of such noble deeds as have been commemorated here today, and the occasion demands that reference be made to some of them as kindred acts to share these honours.

Boonesborough, the site of the first fort worthy of the name in Kentucky, the seat of the first legislative assembly in the valley of the Ohio, the headquarters of the great Transylvania Company which helped to plant civilization in the transmontane wilderness, the first safe home for women in our State, and the place selected by Boone, the pioneer, for a great city that was to endure forever, has passed away like the ocean wave that leaves no trace behind. There is nothing in the beautiful landscape on the Kentucky River, in Madison County, to indicate where Boonesborough stood, and yet it lives in the memory of the three young girls who were captured there by the Indians in 1776. They were Jemima Boone, and Betsy and Frances Galloway, daughters of Colonel Daniel Boone and Colonel Richard Calloway.

They fought the Indians with the paddles of the canoe in which they were captured until overcome, and then in their forced march through the untrodden woods, in defiance of the uplifted *tomahawk*, they marked their way with bits of their clothing and with bent and broken twigs, so that their course might be found by those they knew would follow for their rescue. What could be more appropriate or patriotic than to purchase the site of this vanished town, surround it with a picket fence, replant it with forest trees, and erect on it a facsimile of the old fort! The cabins might be used for the habitation of those who cared for the property, for the storing of relics of the pioneer period, and for such other wants as time might develop, while the grounds, enlivened by deer and other wild animals, might be the paradise of visiting parties. Thus arranged it might become a kind of pioneer Mecca instead of perpetuating the cheerless waste it now presents.

The act of Mary Wood, a delicate young girl of seventeen, in killing with an axe a savage who had invaded her home near Stanford in 1782, entitles her to rank among the heroines of her day.

In 1783 Mrs. Nathaniel Hart rode on horseback through the dark forest from White Oak Station to Logan's, a distance of fifty miles, not only to administer upon the estate of her husband, who had been killed the year before by the Indians, but to meet there and aid and comfort twenty-three other unfortunates who had likewise been made widows by the Indians during that terrible year of 1782.

Mrs. John Merrill, of Nelson County, should never pass from the memory of those who honour brave deeds. In 1787 a party of Indians attacked her house, and her husband was disabled by them when he opened the door to see what caused the outside disturbance. The Indians then attempted to hew down the door with their *tomahawks*, but Mrs. Merrill stood by with an axe, the favourite weapon among pioneer women, and as their heads appeared through the hole hewed in the door killed or wounded four of them. Two others then attempted to descend the low, broad, wooden chimney, but Mrs. Merrill threw her only feather bed on the fire, which so smothered them that she easily dispatched them with her axe. All the Indians, including those she had wounded, then left her mistress of the fortress.

In 1789 an abandoned wretch, who was a fugitive from justice in the older settlements, and who lived in the new country by plundering his neighbours, made his appearance at the home of Samuel Davis, near Whitley's Station, in Lincoln County. Mr. Davis and some neighbours were then in pursuit of the miscreant, of which he was ignorant. When the renegade entered the house, Mrs. Davis invited him to a seat and offered him a drink of whisky. The fellow suspecting nothing, set his gun against the wall, and, while swallowing his drink, Mrs. Davis seized his gun, cocked it, and pointing it at him ordered him to remain seated. And thus she held him at the muzzle of his own gun until her husband and the party in pursuit of him arrived and took him in charge.

Innes' Bottom, near Frankfort, has been made famous by the act of two pioneer women, each of whom was named Elizabeth Cook. Among the settlers here were Jesse and Hosea Cook, with their wives and children. In 1792 they were attacked by a large body of Indians. Jesse Cook was killed at the first fire and Hosea mortally wounded.

He made out, however, to get into the house, where he expired so soon as his wife had closed the door. The Indians then tried to break down the door of the house, in which were the two women with their children. Failing in this they made several attempts to fire the house by flashing powder in their gun-pans. The fire was at first extinguished by the women with water, then with eggs, and finally with the blood-saturated clothing of Hosea Cook lying dead on the floor. The Indians having thus been baffled in their efforts for a considerable time, and fearing the coming of the whites upon them, left the heroic widows to undisturbed sorrow over the bodies of their dead husbands. And thus I might go on relating the heroic deeds of Kentucky women until the day were ended and the shadows of night were upon us.

The Parts of the Siege of Bryant's Omitted in this Address.

The narrative of the siege of Bryant's Station was dropped by me at the failure of the first assault by the Indians. To complete the story it would be necessary to take it up where it was suspended and pursue it to the close of the events which followed, embracing the arrival of the mounted men from Lexington, the return to Lexington of the footmen who could not enter the fort, the attempt of Simon Girty to negotiate a surrender which his arms could not accomplish, the characteristic speech of Girty and the witty reply of Aaron Reynolds, the raising of the siege and the departure of the Indians, the gathering of the pioneers from other stations to the site of Bryant's, the pursuit of the Indians and the disastrous Battle of the Blue Licks. The want of time, however, will not permit even a partial presentation of these subsequent events, important as they may be to the completion of the story.

Fortunately they have all been more or less fully set forth in our histories, which was not the case with the first act in the siege of Bryant's Station, in which the women were principally concerned. I have confined what I had to say to this first act of the siege because there was room there for the presentation of new matter, and because it afforded the opportunity to fill an important gap in our history with the neglected names of pioneer mothers and daughters who, at the risk of their own lives, supplied a besieged station with water by going to the spring for it within point blank range of hundreds of rifles in the hands of blood-thirsty savages. This noble act, in my opinion, entitled them to especial consideration on this occasion, and hence they have been made the principal subject of my address.

Our poet, William D. Gallagher, had in his mind just such women as we have been honouring here today when he wrote his stirring verses entitled *The Mothers of the West!* These singularly appropriate lines, written more than fifty years ago, (as at time of first publication), seem with prophetic vision to have anticipated our exercises here today, and with them I shall close my address, already too long drawn out:

1

The Mothers of our Forest-Land!
Stout-hearted dames were they;
With nerve to wield the battle-brand,
And join the border fray.
Our rough land had no braver
In its days of blood and strife—
Aye, ready for severest toil,
Aye, free to peril life.

2

The Mothers of our Forest-Land!
On old Kentucky's soil,
How shared they, with each dauntless band,
War's tempest and life's toil!
They shrank not from the foeman,
They quail'd not in the fight,
But cheer'd their husbands through the day,
And sooth'd them through the night.

3

The Mothers of our Forest-Land!
Their bosoms pillow'd Men;
And proud were they by such to stand
In hammock, fort, or glen;
To load the sure old rifle—
To run the leaden ball—
To watch a battling husband's place,
And fill it should he fall.

4

The Mothers of our Forest-Land!
Such were their daily deeds;
Their monument—where does it stand?

Their epitaph—who reads?
No bravers dames had Sparta—
No nobler matrons Rome—
Yet who or lauds or honours them,
Ev'n in their own green home?

5

The Mothers of our Forest-Land!
They sleep in unknown graves;
And had they borne and nursed a band
Of ingrates, or of slaves,
They had not been more neglected;
But their graves shall yet be found,
And their monuments dot here and there
"The Dark and Bloody Ground!"

THE WOMEN OF BRYANT'S STATION

Original Poem.

By Major Henry T. Stanton, Member of the Filson Club.

For meet companionship to man,
With life and love in common,
And for perfection of his plan,
God's afterthought was—woman.
Whilst Adam slept, from out his side
Was wrought this final feature,
To give His imaged Self a bride—
A reproducing creature.

Then flowers bloomed in Eden's wild,
And birds and waters greeted,
And every scene the eye beguiled,
And earth was all completed.
The crowning act of God was done,
The King of Kings had rested,
And man and woman, two as one,
With royal right invested.

What had been life to Him alone,
On mountain, vale, and river,
Had Adam held his mighty throne,
To live and rule forever?
What had been power, love, or life
To him in isolation,

Major Henry T. Stanton

But for God's afterthought—a wife,
His last and best creation?
THE WOMEN OF BRYANT'S STATION.

From her the royal scions came
That hold the world in leashes;
The lines that set all life aflame,
The God-like human species—
These be the hands that sway the earth,
That constant point its steerage,
That bring their royalty to birth
And proudly hold its peerage.

God drew no parting line between—
To favour one or other—
The King is master, and the Queen
Is mistress and is mother.
The right to reign and rule this sphere
Is granted to the human,
There is no sex in soul, and here
It may be man or woman.

Throughout the ages that are dead,
With all their glaring errors,
Most legends show how men have led
The bloody way to terrors.
Great battles fought with brand and blade
That live for us in story,
To man's eternal shame are made
His monuments of glory.

The robbers of an older day,
Reliant on their power,
Who through the weaker cut their way,
Were heroes of the hour.
They held their tenures wide and grand
Through right of brigand forces,
And kept dominion of the land
By base and brutal courses.

Their names are carved on granite stones
Set up in honoured places,
Above the ashes and the bones
Of slaughtered feebler races;

But nowhere on this field of fame
The arch of ether under
Is carven any woman's name
Who dyed her blade for plunder.
And few on earth have lived to see
In deathless lines of story
The woman's real history
And charter right to glory.
But here and there across the lands
Her fame has wide extended,
When boldly and with willing hands
Her home has been defended.

There is no brutal force in her,
No muscle built upon her,
But courage in her blood runs clear
When virtue calls or honour.
And sturdy men who meet in war
As valiant foemen—brothers,
Are debtors deep for all they are
To proud and fearless mothers.

No need to cite a woman's acts
In common scription worded,
Her courage shows in living facts,
Unnoted, unrecorded.
In what she does, how brave so e'er,
She flaunts no glaring feature,
But careless shows with danger near
The highest moral nature.

Sometimes, when ocean's beaten shores
Are lined with waiting wreckers,
Grace Darling plies her ashen oars
Across the angry breakers;
Sometimes, in battles' blast and blare,
When wounded men are dying,
A Florence Nightingale is there,
Her hands of mercy plying.

But yesterday, when death was rife
In madly raging water,
A mother freely gave her life

To save her helpless daughter.
Such acts as these are not for fame,
Nor done for self-revealing—
They come uncalled, in mercy's name,
From noblest human feeling.

A hundred years and more have sped
Since here at Bryant's Station
The woman nature grandly shed
Its lustre on creation.
A simple act it seemed to those,
The sister, mother, daughter,
Who in the front of savage foes
Went down this path for water.

These lands about were virgin then,
No plough had scarred their faces,
And canebrake rank and forest fen
Usurped these grassy places.
On every side the dark trees stood
To cast their leaf-made shadows;
No shining axe had shorn the wood,
No bloom stood over meadows.

Some pioneers had made their way
Across the rugged border,
To give this spot the light of day
And bring its soil to order;
Some iron men who braved the wild,
Through rude, untrodden courses,
To find where kindly nature smiled
Amid her rich resources.

Here, with their little household bands,
Were flecked their cabin quarters,
New castles built by knightly hands
For noble wives and daughters.
No feudal lord restrained their toil,
Their strong limbs held no bondage,
They came as masters of the soil,
Its waters, fruits, and frondage.

But though they claimed and held it all
With holder's right invested,

The red-skinned aboriginal
Their brave advance contested.
From out beyond Ohio's bend,
Kentucky's leaf-shade under,
He made his predatory trend
For murder and for plunder.

To shield themselves from raiding bands
That left this savage nation,
Those pioneers with stalwart hands
Erected Bryant's Station.
You know the story—how they came
For mad rapine and slaughter,
And how our women went to fame
Along this path for water.

In history, though briefly told,
Is found the graphic story
That proves the woman-nature gold
And radiant of glory.
Here, fronting death, in battle's fen,
For love's divine relation,
They brought the draught to thirsting men
That saved old Bryant's Station.

And meet it is, when years have passed,
That by these living waters
A noting stone should come at last
As tribute from their daughters.
How good it is, that where this spring
Flows down to join the river,
There now should stand a speaking thing
To tell their fame forever.

Thank God that in creation's mould,
When He conceived the human,
There lay enough of purest gold
To form the perfect woman.
Thank God that in His afterthought,
Through kindness to his creature,
His mighty hand with cunning wrought
This last, this crowning feature.

Through every way of human life

That mortal man is going,
From mother, daughter, sister, wife,
This courage high is showing,
And to all thirsting souls on earth,
From every clime and quarter,
The woman—best and fairest birth—
Is nobly bringing water.

PROFESSOR GEORGE W. RANCK

The Story of Bryan's Station

(Regarding alternative spelling see footnote 5 on page 46)

AN ADDRESS

BY PROFESSOR GEORGE W. RANCK,

MEMBER OF THE FILSON CLUB.

Madam Regent and Ladies of the Lexington Chapter of the
Daughters of the American Revolution, Ladies and Gentlemen, I have
been honoured by the Lexington Chapter of the Daughters of the
American Revolution with the commission to write for this notable
occasion[1] *The Story of Bryan's Station.* The ladies gave me no easy task,
for while much of the material that has come down to us on this
subject is good, all of it is fragmentary, some of it is confused and inac-
curate, and not a little is mere repetition embellished by an exuberant
fancy. It is for these reasons partly that Bryan's Station has not taken
the place it deserves in general American history, a place from which,
let us hope, it will no longer be missing after the events of this auspi-
cious day.

I have tried in this address to remove these blemishes and to overcome these disadvantages. To do this I have gone back to original
sources of information entirely—to eye-witnesses of the events and
actors in the scenes at Bryan's Station, and to authorities who actually lived when the pioneers lived, who knew them personally and
received their facts directly from them.

If this address, therefore, has any merit it is mainly due to the use of
contemporary evidence which furnishes the strongest material from
which history can be written; to the fact that the writer has conscien-
tiously endeavoured to make it accurate, impartial, and reliable, and

1. As the date of the anniversary of the event commemorated August 16th fell this
year (1896) on Sunday, the dedicatory exercises at Bryan's Station were, for conven-
ience, held on Tuesday, August 18, 1896.

because it is the first attempt that has ever been made to give to our literature a full, complete, and consecutive

STORY OF BRYAN'S STATION.

An eloquent and perpetual reminder of the coming of the pioneers to the Bluegrass Region of Kentucky is an English name. In 1773, when the McAfees penetrated for the first time to these luxuriant depths, an elk was killed that so surpassed all others they had seen that his grandly branching antlers were set up as a trophy on the bank of a new-found stream, and from that day to this the once unheard of water has been known by the beautiful name of "Elkhorn."[2]

The earliest known explorers identified with the north fork of this romantic stream, and with the ground now known as "Bryan's Station," came here in 1774 and 1775, and included John Floyd, James Douglas, and Hancock Taylor, three deputy surveyors of Fincastle County, Virginia, of which Kentucky was then a part; William Bryan, a hunter from that section of North Carolina now known as Rowan County, and John Ellis, a Virginia veteran of the French and Indian wars.[3] The land they sought was all that even the land-craving heart of the Anglo-Saxon could desire, and claims were located, surveys made, and temporary improvements were started.

But the day of possession was not yet. The explorers were suddenly forced to abandon their camp, which remained abandoned for years, for war had broken out between the outraged Ohio Indians and the colony of Virginia, and it had barely ended when the great struggle for American independence commenced. The experiences of the adventurous spirits we have named strikingly illustrate the perils of the Kentucky wilderness at this time. They all endured almost incredible privations and sufferings, all of them were wounded by the Indians, and three out of the five met death at their hands.[4]

In 1779 that remarkable and mischievous land law of Virginia was enacted which turned such a tide of immigration into Kentucky, and

---

2. McAfee's *Pioneer Sketches.*

3. Henderson's *Journal*; see also Fayette records, Denham *v.* Johnson, in which William Bryan proves settlement of John Ellis on North Elkhorn.

4. Taylor was killed in Madison County in 1774, Bryan in Fayette in 1780, and Floyd in Jefferson in 1783. Douglas died in Bourbon in 1793, and Ellis in Fayette in 1797. Floyd secured an immense amount of Kentucky land, and Fayette County records credit Ellis with the enormous number of ninety-three thousand acres, variously located. Ellis and Floyd both served in the Continental Army after the visit to the North Elkhorn region detailed above.

permanent settlements were made for the first time within the present limits of Fayette County. One of these was Bryan's Station. It was founded by four Bryan[5] brothers from North Carolina, William, Morgan, James, and Joseph, of whom the above-mentioned William was the leading spirit, and with them was William Grant, who, like the leader, had married a sister of Daniel Boone. All five were elderly but stalwart woodsmen, and as each was blessed with a great family of children, in accordance with a striking feature of the day, and as the children themselves were nearly all grown, they felt prepared for straggling Indians at least, as with dogs and flint-lock rifles, pack-horses and cows, they set out from the valley of the Yadkin.

At the Cumberland River they were joined by two land hunters they accidentally met there, Cave Johnson and William Tomlinson, from Virginia, who for their better protection made the journey with the party, and helped to build the station when the trip ended.[6] They all came by way of Boonesborough, where they stopped to replenish their supply of corn, and from that fort, after a laborious march, they came to the North Elkhorn Creek, where they made a final halt at a spot about five miles northeast of the little stockaded settlement of Lexington. Here, in the very heart of the neutral ground of the Northern and Southern Indians, in the centre of their choicest game park where all might hunt, but where no tribe might remain, and in that section of it which Bancroft describes as "the matchless valley of the Elkhorn," was Bryan's Station planted.

How little did these rich acres cost in gold how much did they cost in suffering and in blood! The new station was quickly built. It was a rude and solitary habitation, but as strong as it was rude. It consisted at first of twelve or fourteen cabins of logs with the bark on, with roofs of roughest clapboards, and provided with chimneys of sticks and clay,

---

5. We give the name as it was used by most of the members of the family in Kentucky at that time, though it was then known as Bryant" also. The certificates issued by the Land Commissioners at the session of their court held at the station in December, 1779, and January, 1780, called the family "Bryan" and the locality "Bryant's Station." (See Bryan and Owens v. Wallace, Fayette records.) And this precedent was followed by the Court of Appeals. (See same case.) In the official reports of the Battle of the Blue Licks, August, 1782, Boone gives the station name without the "t," while Caldwell (British) and Levi Todd both use that letter. John Filson, 1784, prints it one way on his map and the other way in his book, and so on from the settlement of the station down to the present time both forms of the name have been used in court records and by historians and the public.

6. *Autobiography of Cave Johnson.* He and Tomlinson went back to Virginia in a few weeks, but both returned.

46

but unlighted by one pane of glass, and all arranged as a hollow square by the aid of great pickets made of the trunks of trees split in two and planted firmly in the ground. And the whole, green as the forest from which it had been hewed, was fashioned by the axe and put together by wooden pegs and pins without the help of a nail or hinge of iron. The station was more noticeable at this time for its situation than for its size. It stood on an elevated point[7] that had been cleared of trees big enough to screen an enemy, and which tapered steeply down to the southern bank of the heavily wooded creek.

At the foot of the hill which hid it from the station, and facing the creek, was a spring of almost ice-cold water that issued from a ledge of rocks that long jutted from the hillside, but which was covered by wild vegetation and thick primeval mosses, and the clear little stream that came from it, uniting with another like it, flowed unseen into the creek through a thicket of waving cane. This spring, which had much to do with determining the location of the fort, [8] was destined through the heroism of Kentucky women to become the most famous fountain of the western wilderness. A footpath, zigzagging through the freshly made stumps of trees and past some saplings of dogwood and pawpaw, led down from the station to this spring, while a much broader track sloped from the main gate on the southeastern side of the stockade to a road a little distance away, and nearly fronting the fort, that was a priceless boon to the pioneers.

It seemed an ancient product of human skill, but was, in fact, a "trace," hard and firm, made by the buffaloes alone which had thundered over it for a thousand years in their journeys to the Salt Licks. Nearby was a clearing planted in corn, but all else but the hill itself—the forests, the cane-brakes, the wilderness stream, the wild rye, the pea-vine, and the white clover—was unchanged by the hand of man. The settlers were very busy, for they had to depend upon themselves alone for the commonest comforts and necessaries of life. Pots and skillets and a few ordinary implements they did possess, but nearly everything else they had to make, from slab tables to buffalo tallow dips, from hand mills to deerskin *moccasins*. And hunting seemed never

---

7. Marshall's *History of Kentucky*. John Bradford's *Notes on the Early Settlement of Kentucky*.

8. A spring was such a necessity of early pioneer life that it nearly always determined the location of a settlement. It was a spring that caused the erection of the cabins at Harrodsburg, Boonesborough, Georgetown, Lexington, and a multitude of other forts and stations in Kentucky.

to stop, for the settlers lived on wild game, and times were bad indeed at Bryan's Station when the ranger came back without his usual load. Thanks to the blow inflicted by the genius of Clark in his Vincennes campaign, the Indians halted for a little season in their work of murder, and game could be had without the constant risk of life, and more immigrants found their way to the Bluegrass Region in the fall of 1779. Some of them settled at Bryan's, greatly to the delight of its lonely little band, and among them were Stephen Frank, Nicholas Tomlinson, Thomas Bell, David Jones, James Hogan, Huttery Lee, and Daniel Wilcoxen. Others under the leadership of Colonel John Grant, of North Carolina, and Captain William Ellis, of Virginia, went five miles further toward the spot where Paris now stands and established Grant's Station.[9]

As the new settlers were mostly kinsmen or friends of those at Bryan's, and as neighbours were not overly plentiful, a trace was quickly cut and cleared between the two forts, and it, like the buffalo trace to Lexington, now gave signs of human travel.

Bryan's Station was unusually animated in December, 1779, and January, 1780, in spite of the bitterly cold weather, as the Commissioners appointed by Virginia to settle land claims held their court within its snow-covered walls, and the pioneers gathered in to get the certificates that meant so much to them, for these documents secured to each holder four hundred acres of land actually settled, and a pre-emption right to purchase at the State price a thousand acres or less adjoining his settlement, provided the settlement had been made before January 1, 1778, on unappropriated land, to which no other had a legal right. Daniel Boone, Simon Kenton, Robert Patterson, the Todds, Ellis, McConnells, and many others of the early pioneers of Fayette County visited Bryan's Station at this time. It was while

---

9. Colonel Grant, who was a Revolutionary soldier, was one of the most active of the pioneers. He and Captain Ellis seem to have first met in the Continental Army, to which they both returned when their settlement was broken up by Byrd in 1780. They both came back to Kentucky and settled permanently, Ellis in the winter of 1781 and Grant in the spring of 1782 (not in 1784, as Collins has it). Colonel Grant died at his home on the Licking, where he had erected salt works years before. There were five of the Grants, including William, at Bryan's, and all came from the Shallow Ford of the Yadkin, and all were conspicuous as frontiersmen. Israel was with Boone in his pursuit of the Indians who killed Edward Boone, brother of Daniel, in October, 1781. Samuel Grant was killed by the Indians near the Ohio in 1794. William was wounded in the tragic hunt on the Elkhorn. Squire was State Senator from Boone County in 1801.

this court was in session that the Bryans, who had rested secure in the belief that they were the owners of the station land by right of settlement, met the first of a series of discouragements that caused them to abandon the place. Their settlement was found to be within the limits of a survey made in July, 1774, for William Preston, then surveyor of Fincastle County, Virginia, who had already traded it off to Joseph Rogers, also a resident of Virginia.[10]

This misfortune, a long spell of terribly severe weather, and other adverse circumstances made the winter a gloomy one at Bryan's. As the season advanced the little store of corn was exhausted, owing to the presence of newcomers, who increased the consumption of it and had arrived too late to plant for themselves. So there was no bread, and even meat was scarce, for the larger game went further away as settlers increased.

The spring of 1780 came, and with it came the Indians, as they always did at that season of the year. All the traces were infested with them, and several hunters had already been killed, when the salt gave out both at Lexington and at Bryan's, and as salt was indispensable, a party of men made up from both places started for Bullitt's Lick, near Salt River, to get some. But they had hardly passed the little cluster of stockaded cabins called Leestown, and reached the bank of the Kentucky River, when they were suddenly attacked by Indians, who killed Stephen Frank, and wounded Nicholas Tomlinson, William Bryan, and several others of the party, who, however, quickly recovered, but the expedition had to be abandoned. Frankfort, subsequently settled near the site of this occurrence, is said to have taken its name from the unfortunate hunter killed that day.

More Indians than ever now beset the traces and the fort, and neither the pioneers nor their stock could go beyond the clearing without danger; meat grew scarcer still, and hunting parties, to avoid the savages, had to slip out of the station before daybreak, make a wide circuit and return at night. When a man went out at this time he was never certain that he would ever get back.

About the 20th of May this year (1780[11]) meat was so badly needed that twelve mounted men rode from the station in quest of game to some woods near where Georgetown now stands. There they divided,

---

10. Deposition of Joseph Rogers in 1791, Fayette County records. The patent says: "Granted to Joseph Rogers and John Seabury;" Bledsoe *v.* Tandy. Preston was never in Kentucky. He died in 1783 in what is now Montgomery County, Virginia.
11. Several writers, including Collins, have incorrectly given the year as 1781.

with the understanding that one party under William Bryan, and another under James Hogan, should range down the Elkhorn—each party taking a side—and meet at night at the mouth of Cane Run. Soon after they parted Hogan and his men were pursued by Indians, and, abandoning a led horse brought along to carry game, they distanced the savages and galloped back to the station. Early the next morning Hogan, with reinforcements, went to the relief of Bryan's party, which had camped at the place agreed upon, but they arrived too late to prevent disaster. The Indians had used the captured packhorse, which was provided with a bell, to lead the other party into an ambuscade, and had defeated the hunters, mortally wounding William Bryan and severely wounding William Grant, when Hogan's band rode up and finally routed the savages in turn.

In this last fight one of the Indians was killed and scalped, and three of the white men were wounded. One of the wounded was David Jones, after whom "David's Fork," a tributary of the Elkhorn, was named.[12] He was shot through the middle of the chest, but survived. The suffering hunters, supported in their saddles, were brought to the station, where protracted anxiety gave way to successive feelings of joy, sympathy, and fear as the faint and bleeding little party filed slowly through the gate. William Bryan, who had been mangled by three bullets, was carried to his cabin in a dying condition, and before the dawn of another morning the unfortunate woodsman expired. And then, in the midst of sorrow and great depression, while four wounded men required attention, and with every male mourner carrying a rifle, occurred the first funeral at Bryan's Station.

No church bell tolled as the little train went carefully over the rocks and logs where the buffalo trace crossed the creek, and there was no music but the rippling of the forest stream when the settlers halted in the woods on the other side opposite the station. A good man made a simple prayer, and William Bryan was laid to rest under the spreading branches of an oak which stood at his head, with his initials deeply cut into the bark.

The Bryans had talked of leaving the station as soon as they found that they were not the owners of the land, and now after the death of their leader they were more inclined to abandon it than ever. One more event settled the matter, for they barely escaped destruction. On

---

12. The stream was first known as "David Jones' Fork," and afterward familiarly shortened to "Davy's Fork," but for nearly a century has held to the more dignified appellation of "David's Fork." See depositions, Fayette County records.

the 22nd of June, Colonel Byrd, of the British Army, at the head of one of the largest and most formidable bodies of Indians and Canadians that had ever invaded Kentucky, captured Ruddle's Station in the present Harrison County, and immediately took Martin's also, which was only a few miles from Bryan's.[13] Consternation reigned in all the log forts, for the invaders had brought to Kentucky for the first time the one thing the pioneers dreaded—artillery.

Grant's Station was instantly evacuated, much to the disgust of scouting Indians, who managed, however, to kill some of the rapidly retreating garrison, and then pushed on to Bryan's, where they seized many horses, ruined much of the growing corn, and were confidently expecting the arrival of the army, when Colonel Byrd, either through fear of the sudden falling of the waters of the Licking, from disgust at the utter disregard of his authority by his wild allies, or from horror at their atrocities, hastily retreated, and the station that seemed doomed to immediate destruction was saved as by a miracle.

The Bryans and others from the same State were now utterly discouraged, and determined to return to North Carolina. But it was no easy matter to get away, with land selling for a song, and everything else enormously high, and with women, children, household goods, and provisions to move, after the Indians had stolen nearly all the horses. In July corn was selling at one hundred and twenty dollars per bushel in Continental currency, and one man was known to have given as much as nine hundred acres of pre-emption land for a horse.

All the wounded hunters in the station had time to get well before the arrangements for the trip were completed, but the emigrants were ready at last, and early one morning at the close of the month of August, 1780, the pack-horses were loaded, farewells were said to the few who remained, the conch shell was blown, the train moved off on the old buffalo trace, and the Bryans and their party abandoned the station

---

13. Ruddle's Fort was about a mile and a quarter above the site now known as Lair's Station, while Martin's was still closer to Bryan's, as it was on Stoner Creek in Bourbon County. It was about five miles from Ruddle's.

14. Morgan Bryan, one of the four brothers, in a deposition before James Trotter, taken March 10, 1795, refers to the movements of the Bryans and others in May, 1780, and says, "All of whom and myself removed from the Kentucky country in the August following, and none of us returned, as far as I know, before the year 1784." Daniel Bryan and George Bryan depose that they left in 1780, but state that they returned at a later date than 1784, while Samuel Bryan simply deposes that he remained at the station until the summer of 1780. See Fayette records, Bryan and Owens v. Wallace; Bledsoe v. Tandy, and other suits.

forever.[14] They had been there but little more than a year, but troubles and privations had made the time seem infinitely longer. Some years after this, when the war was over, and pioneers could live outside of the prison-like forts, members of this family and party came back to other lands they had taken up in Fayette County, but to Bryan's Station they returned no more.

So, at the beginning of the autumn of 1780, only a few of the cabins at Bryan's Station were occupied, and the place seemed about to be entirely deserted when its prospects brightened. Clark's expedition against the Piqua Indians, immediately after Byrd's invasion, restored confidence; immigrants began to pour into the country, and a number of them from Virginia settled at Bryan's, making the station stronger than ever. Among them were John Ellis, one of the original explorers, with his family and negroes; three Craigs, Elijah, John, and Jeremiah; Joseph Stucker and relatives, and John Martin, John Suggett, and several Hendersons, Herndons, and Mitchells.

Later in the fall came Mr. Williams, of North Carolina, with his young son Ellison, and about the same time arrived Robert Johnson,[15] brother of Cave Johnson, from Beargrass, near the present Louisville, with his family, including his infant son, Richard M., born at that place, and afterward distinguished as a soldier and Vice-President. The newcomers added more cabins to the station, increased its comforts and conveniences, and, what was of vital importance, increased its strength, for now since the fall of Martin's and Ruddle's it was the most exposed of all the stations north of the Kentucky River. Lexington was superior, but it was mainly because her founders had the forethought to include a splendid spring within her walls, an advantage, strange to say, that none of the other stations enjoyed.

When the winter came on the Indians left the settlers to fight the snow and ice and starvation, but they were back again as soon as the spring of 1781 brought pleasant weather. Before the dogwood bloomed they had crept up to the station and killed a man who was on the lookout while Daniel Wilcoxen ploughed the corn, and it was only by a lucky accident that Wilcoxen escaped with his life. June opened with another tragedy, for Huttery Lea was killed while trying to give his horse grass outside of the walls so incessantly watched by the skulking foe. His horse was shot and he himself was scalped, dying while yet a youth.

---

15. *Autobiography of Cave Johnson*. Both of the Johnson brothers had to go to Virginia in the spring of 1782, and did not return until the fall of that year.

Both of these victims of the Indians were buried by the side of William Bryan in the rude station graveyard across the creek. But the settlement survived in spite of everything, and the hearts of the inmates were strengthened when the news was brought in December that a whole congregation of Virginians had arrived at Gilbert's Creek,[16] and that a number of old friends and neighbours who formed part of it would settle near them in the coming spring. Not only were more strong arms needed, but all hungered and thirsted for news from their far-distant old home, for letters were few and hard to get, and not a single newspaper was published in the entire Kentucky wilderness.

The winter was monotonous, but the spring of 1782 was marked by an early omen of a tragic year, for the station was shocked on the 23rd of March by the news of Estill's defeat, brought by two survivors of the fatal engagement. One was William Irvine, helpless from three gunshot wounds, and the other was Joseph Proctor, who had rescued him after the most desperate and gallant exertions. In April, about two weeks after this incident, the expected Virginia families arrived from Gilbert's Creek, reinforcing Bryan's and other Bluegrass forts to some extent, but mainly uniting to settle on David's Fork.[17] None, however, were distant from Bryan's, where their leader, Captain William Ellis, and some of his riflemen were destined soon to gather.

Bryan's Station was at its best in the summer of 1782. It then included about forty cabins with clapboard roofs, all of which sloped inwardly, and like all the larger pioneer forts in Kentucky was a parallelogram in shape, with a block-house at each angle, and every space not occupied by the back or outside wall of a cabin was filled in with pointed log pickets twelve feet high. Commencing a little distance from the northeastern brow of the hill overlooking the creek, it ran back two hundred yards in length by fifty yards in width, and was provided with two big gates that swung on enormous wooden hinges one of the gates being on the southeastern side nearest the buffalo trace, which long afterward developed into the Bryan Station Turnpike.[18]

On the outside and close to the palisades were several cabins, in one of which lived James Morgan, his wife and one infant child, and

---

16. Near Lancaster, Kentucky. See *The Travelling Church*, published 1891.

17. Now known as the Chilesburg neighbourhood. *History of Fayette County, Kentucky.*

18. It remained a "dirt road" until 1859, when the five miles from the city limits of Lexington were macadamized.

there were other structures that sheltered tanning vats, rude contrivances for making rope and other absolutely necessary articles. The live stock had increased, more land had been cleared and fenced, a vegetable garden was flourishing, and a hundred acres of full grown corn extended along one side of the buffalo trace past the fort and down to the forest-covered bank of the creek. Trees still thickly lined the other side of the trace, making it now a narrow lane. There was a heavy growth of hemp west and north of the present old brick residence which stands on the ground, then clear of everything but stumps and tall weeds; wild rye and a thicket of lofty cane, in which a man on horseback could hide, covered the marshy bottom between the hillside and the creek in the neighbourhood of the spring, so that the station, though it stood in the midst of cleared and elevated land, was rimmed around at no great distance by luxuriant vegetation.

Such was Bryan's Station before the sun set on the 15th of August, 1782, but there was excitement in the little garrison of forty-four riflemen, and among the women and children, by the time the bear grease lamps and buffalo tallow dips were lighted, for a messenger had galloped up with the news that Captain John Holder, with men from his own station, from McGee's, and Strode's, had been defeated at the Upper Blue Licks by a band of Indians he had been pursuing, who had committed depredations and captured children at Hoy's Station in the present Madison County. The word was for the settlers to rendezvous at Hoy's.[19] Lexington had already been notified and was preparing to go and hunt down the savages, and now the garrison at Bryan's hurried to get ready to do the same, which was exactly what a wily foe had commissioned his advance guard to effect, with a view to the destruction of both places,[20] for one of the largest forces that had ever come against the settlements was even then at their very gates.

The northwestern tribes, though often at variance with each other, never forgot that Kentucky was the common hunting ground of them

19. Hoy's Station, which had then (1782) been established about a year, was close to the site of the present Foxtown, in Madison County, and as Holder's was on the Kentucky River, only two miles from Boonesborough, the alarm soon reached him. In his pursuit he increased his party first at McGee's Station, which was on Cooper's Run, in Fayette County, three miles from Boonesborough, and then at Strode's, which was two miles from the present Winchester, and then the principal settlement of what is now Clark County. "Strode's Road" is still a reminder of the old station.
20. Holder was defeated on the 14th or 15th of August; and if the settlers could be drawn away to Hoy's, Bryan's would not only be without a garrison itself but it could obtain no aid from the neighbouring stations, as they too would be depleted.

all, and their inveterate hatred of the pioneer intruders upon it had been repeatedly worked by the British to their own advantage. Such was now the case. Early in August the British Commandant of the Northwest, Lieutenant-Governor Henry Hamilton, whose headquarters were at Detroit, had ordered Captain William Caldwell to collect militia and Indians and "destroy the rebel settlements south of the Ohio."[21] Caldwell,[22] who seems to have been a militia officer of foreign birth and a Tory, if not an actual renegade, gathered one company of Tory and Canadian rangers, and figured as the official and ostensible head of the movement, though its real leader was the notorious Simon Girty,[23] who had been captured by the savages when a child and adopted by them, and had finally become an Indian in everything but complexion, and was a power both in the council house and on the warpath.

A grand conference of the dusky allies of the Crown, to consider the invasion of Kentucky, was held at old Chillicothe,[24] about three miles northwest of the present city of Xenia, Ohio, and the best known of the Shawnee towns or camping places in the Miami country, and here, mainly through the influence of Girty, the tribes again united to make another and a supreme effort to drive the whites from their ancient domain forever. A force was immediately organized for this purpose, and included quotas of warriors from the Shawanese, Wyandot, Huron, and five or six other tribes, in whose overshadowing numbers the handful of militia was lost, and the authority of Caldwell seems to have been even more completely ignored than was that of

---

21. Haldimand MSS., Ottawa, Canada. Sir Frederick Haldimand was Governor of Canada from 1778 to 1784.

22. Caldwell figured conspicuously at Sandusky in June (1782). A prejudiced writer makes him the inactive captain of a company of Tory militia disguised as Indians at the Battle of Fallen Timber, in 1794. Shortly after this, when the British delivered up the military posts of the Northwest, he settled at Amherstburg (formerly Maiden), Canada, along with Byrd, Girty, and McKee.

23. See *Girty the White Indian* in *Magazine of American History* for March, 1886, which the author claims as the first attempt in more than a century to give Girty's life after a careful and unprejudiced study of the most reliable original authorities, both British and American.

24. This ancient camping ground of the Shawanese and favourite rendezvous of the savage tribes when on the warpath was near the head of the Little Miami River. Traces led from it to other so-called "towns," including those of the Piqua and Pickaway Indians on the Big Miami.

25. Ruddle remonstrated with Byrd about the barbarities of the Indians. Byrd confessed himself unable to restrain them, saying they so greatly outnumbered the British that he was in their power.

Byrd at Ruddle's and Martin's two years before.[25]

In fact, most of the assembled warriors had participated in that very movement, and, uncontrollable as ever, had chosen a leader of their own, and from this time until the campaign ended Girty had the whole Indian force at his back, and was the real commander and master-spirit of the expedition. He was certainly recognized as such by the pioneers, who mention no other opposing leader, and the British records show that he had already played nearly as prominent a part at Ruddle's when, supported by the savages, he and not Byrd demanded the surrender of the place.[26] Backed by such a force he did not need a commission from Hamilton to make him a leader.

The exact strength of the invading force will never be known. The lowest estimate on the British side[27] puts it at three hundred men, and the highest from one of the best American sources[28] makes it considerably over six hundred. Boone, who was a close personal observer of this matter, and whose written statements are singularly calm and unprejudiced, says at one time that "the Indians exceeded four hundred," and at another time[29] that "the Indians and Canadians together were about five hundred."[30]

There is every reason to believe that they amounted to about five hundred, but no matter how estimated, by friend or foe, the force appeared overwhelming for the end in view.

Exulting in their strength, unimpeded by baggage of any kind, and equipped only for a very short campaign, during which they expected to live mainly upon the enemy, the warriors started out from the Shawanese camp, speeded down the Little Miami, swarmed across the Ohio in canoes, moved rapidly up the Licking, and, on the night of August 15th,[31] arrived at Bryan's Station and silently settled

---

26. Haldimand Papers. The British governor was not unmindful of the influence Girty exerted among the northwestern tribes. Kiernan says, in Volume 2 of *American Pioneer*, that Girty was armed by Hamilton with a proclamation from his own hand to guarantee pardon and protection to all who would swear allegiance to the Crown.

27. Caldwell. McKee makes the number larger.

28. Bradford, who says, "There were five hundred and sixty Indians and about sixty Canadians and Tories, forming an army of more than six hundred to fight forty-two men."

29. Filson.

30. Marshall adopts Boone's figures as given to Filson. None of the Kentucky historians we mention had access to the British accounts we quote from.

31. Caldwell, Boone, Ellison Williams, Bradford, and Marshall give the 15th as date of arrival. See note on page 72.

themselves about it. Not a single note of warning had been sounded. Boonesborough had been twice besieged, and Martin's and Ruddle's had been destroyed; but no steps seem to have been taken to guard the settlements against surprise, and Girty and his warriors reached the heart of the Bluegrass Region unseen and unchallenged by scout, picket, or sentinel, a circumstance which provoked soon after some exceedingly lively comments from George Rogers Clark. [32]

The whole force took positions either on or near the bank of the creek, and as close to the fort as it could, to be effectually concealed by the tall and abundant vegetation. One detachment was posted among the trees and corn where the trace neared the creek, or about where the southern end of the bridge now is, while the main body buried itself in the canebrake and full grown weeds, "so near the spring," says Marshall, "as to render it useless to the garrison." The Indian leaders were evidently in doubt as to whether the volunteers for the relief of Holder had yet left the fort, and with a view to obtain positive information some scouts were sent before daylight[33] to capture an early riser, or make enough excitement to cause the garrison to expose its strength.

It was one of these pretended stragglers probably who fell before the rifle of James McBride, who, it is claimed, killed the first Indian shot at the siege,[34] and it was at this time that James Morgan escaped from his cabin on the outside of the fort, with his baby strapped to his back, after concealing his wife under a slab of the cabin floor. The thrilling experience of Mrs. Morgan, the burning of the cabin, and the strange meeting of the husband and wife after the Battle of the Blue Licks, is one of the most dramatic features of the siege, [35] The effort of the scouting party not only failed, but, as the captain of the British Rangers admits, was badly managed, and in some unexplained way the quick-witted settlers detected at once the presence of a hidden army, the ambuscade near the spring, and the meaning of the ruse to entice the men away to the relief of Holder.

How they learned this, whether from the tenant of an outside cabin who escaped into the fort, or whether they caught some swift warn-

32. *Virginia State Papers*, Volume 3.

33. Bradford agrees with Caldwell about "the fire of the savages before sunrise."

34. See McBride's *Pioneer Biography*. Captain James McBride was a resident of Lexington and one of the first lot owners. It is not explained how he happened to be at Bryan's Station at this time. He was killed in 1789 while surveying near the Licking, but though shot from his horse he killed an Indian before he was tomahawked.

35. See full account *History of Lexington*.

ing from the Ruddle Station prisoners that the Indians had forced to come along with them, has never been explained.[36] The besiegers, unconscious that their real strength had been discovered, and believing that such an every-day occurrence as the appearance of a few straggling Indians would excite no suspicion of a great force, waited silently and confidently for the departure of the company, or some tell-tale effect of the alarm. But the relief party so fortunately warned did not march, nor did the garrison exhibit itself; but while the enemy waited, the suddenly-aroused and greatly-startled inmates set to work with might and main under the alleged leadership of Captain Elijah Craig [37] to prepare the post for an effective defence, and to beat the savage at his own game of deception.

Thomas Bell and Nicholas Tomlinson immediately undertook the dangerous experiment of riding to Lexington after reinforcements, and made good their escape, owing, perhaps, to the desire of the enemy not to expose his presence, and for the same reason, doubtless, the live stock that congregated every night about the station was allowed to go out unattacked to its familiar range.

The gates had hardly been closed on the messengers when everybody thought of water, for the daily supply had not been brought up, and as it was mid-August all realized in a flash, not only that the fort could not be held without it, but that it must be obtained at once, and by the women, or not had at all. For the men to go to the spring would be to do exactly as the savages desired, and devote the garrison to destruction. If the women went in accordance with their regular early morning custom, the enemy would be confirmed in the delusion that their presence in force was undiscovered, [38] and would withhold their fire to insure the complete success of their plans. The

36. Deposition of Nicholas Hart that he and others captured at Ruddle's in 1780 were forced to accompany the Indians when they marched to Bryan's Station and the Blue Licks. Some of the prisoners were released shortly after the close of the Revolution, but the Ruddles remained in captivity fourteen years, or until the treaty of Greenville in 1794.

37. The identity of the commander of the garrison, who was doubtless only a nominal and temporary leader, is not established on contemporary authority. A later writer, Collins, Volume 2, names an Elijah Craig in this connection, and says that after the siege he removed to what is now Woodford County, Kentucky. Whoever he may have been, he is not to be confused with Elijah Craig, the Baptist preacher, who did not come to Kentucky till 1785, and who died in Scott County in 1808.

38. The Indians evidently believed all this time that their presence in force was entirely unsuspected by the garrison, and all the important contemporary writers convey the impression that they so believed.

suggestion was full of hope, but all the same the savages were known to be mere creatures of impulse, hard to control, and regardless of sex. The effort which promised success might end in a massacre, but the women were convinced of its vital importance, and resolved to go. Never was a demand for heroic self-sacrifice more suddenly made or more simply and sublimely answered.

There was no time for tears and lamentations, only time enough for the gathering of pails, piggins,[39] noggins, and gourds, and for hasty embraces; and as the sun was rising on the memorable Friday of the 16th of August, 1782, the devoted women of Bryan's Station left its protecting walls, and with looks of pretended cheerfulness, but with wildly fluttering hearts, went down the hillside, beyond the reach of the garrison's guns, and gathered at the never-to-be-forgotten spring,[40] in point-blank range of hundreds of the enemy's rifles, and under the very eyes of a swarm of savages who crouched like panthers in close and deadly ambush about them. The coolness and audacity of the movement so completely convinced the Indians that their presence was unsuspected that they allowed neither sign nor sound to betray them, as one after another the women dipped their dripping gourds into the water, filled the pails, carried them up the footpath, and entered the fort.

It was a splendid deed. Think of the lofty character of the women who could endure that sudden parting from the nearest and dearest they had on earth; of the grandeur of their self-sacrifice as they passed down the hillside and out of sight of those protecting walls to which they would return, perhaps, no more forever; of the agony of that long and sickening suspense as they waited their turn at the spring, and of the shining courage that would have done honour to the bearded

39. The piggin was a wooden bucket with one upright stave for a handle. The noggin was a wooden bucket with two upright staves for handles.

40. The identity of this spring as the one so daringly visited by the women of the station at this time is clearly and completely established. It is the only spring mentioned in connection with the siege by the two historians personally familiar with the station at the time, and the only one that answers to their descriptions. Marshall, in his *History of Kentucky*, says "a very fine spring ran from the foot of the point on which the fort stood near the bank of the Elkhorn." Bradford, in his "*Notes*," located the enemy "on the bank of the creek, convenient to the spring, and out of sight of the fort," and then adds that the women got the water from the spring near the ambuscade. The spring now enclosed with a memorial wall is the only one at "the foot of the point" and "near the bank of the Elkhorn." (See a succeeding note.) The location of the spring is certain, no matter how the lines of the fort may have extended.

warrior of any land that they exhibited as going and coming with pretended unconcern they grazed the very precincts of captivity, of torture, and of death. The annals of the world do not contain a more illustrious or a more thoroughly authentic instance of female devotion than this, (See note following), but so common were heroic deeds to the pioneer women of Kentucky, and so well was this one already known, that the historian only mentions it incidentally and in the most matter-of-course way. Such was the mettle of the foremothers of Kentucky, who so grandly made possible the successful defence of Bryan's Station.

> Note:—The genuineness of this incident has never been questioned but once, and then in the shape of an assertion absolutely unsupported and betraying an astonishing ignorance of long-established facts. Albach says, *Western Annals*, published in 1846: "We have it on the best authority, however, that Simon Kenton said this was all romance—by his account there was a covered way to the spring." The value of this assertion will be understood when we state that neither the name of this "best authority" is given, nor the time nor place of the revelation, which was not published until ten years after the death of Kenton, and sixty-four years after the incident happened.
>
> Only one station in all Kentucky ever had even the suggestion of a covered way connected with it, and that was Harrod's, and it is in the shape of an uncertain legend with no satisfactory data to support it. We will add in the interest of historic accuracy that the very nature of the ground at Bryan's Station—a steep hillside—and the distance between the fort and the spring would have made a covered way useless or impossible, nor has the memory of any such thing ever been handed down in any shape by any of the occupants of Bryan's Station, including Joseph Rogers, who saw the fort in 1782, and lived on the spot for fifty years.
>
> Albach's assertion in such questionable shape, and at so late a date as 1846, was not creditable to him in view of the fact that Marshall's description of the spring had then been extant for thirty-four years, for the first volume of his history was published in 1812. Marshall, who was not only a resident of Fayette County in 1782, but was then a surveyor and familiar with the ground, declares it was an open spring, for he described it as

so exposed during the siege as to be practically useless to the garrison, who could not approach it even at night to get water, except at the risk of life, "notwithstanding which," he significantly adds, "it was, however, obtained."

Mr. Roosevelt, in his *Winning of the West* (note, volume 2), accepts the incident as true, but after saying "it is recorded by McClung, a most untrustworthy writer," adopts it from others as authentic tradition. Mr. Roosevelt is in error as to the incident resting on tradition only. It is plain that he did not know it had long been a matter of substantial history also. He evidently knew nothing whatever of Bradford's *Notes*, nor had he noticed that McClung in his preface gives Bradford as his authority for data about the siege. McClung could not have cited better authority, for Bradford was not only a man of high character and ability, but he was in Kentucky the year Bryan's Station was settled, and if afterward he was not an actual participant in the siege, was so early, so long, and so well acquainted with the fort and its defenders as to make his account of the incident contemporary history and absolutely unimpeachable.

Moreover, when it was published in 1826 many of the fort's defenders were still alive to pass judgment upon it if incorrect. They most certainly did not do so, but Ellison E. Williams, who took part in the siege when twelve years old, and was an eye-witness to the incident, confirmed Bradford's statement in a contribution to *Cist's Cincinnati Miscellany*, volume 1. Heroic actions were so common to the pioneer women of Kentucky that but little effort was made to preserve them. Not the half of them has ever been told, and even Bradford treats this one in the most matter-of-course way.

Hope and joy and pride filled the fort as the stout-hearted women returned in safety with the water for which they had risked their lives and all that made life valuable, but the imminence of the danger allowed no time for the display of those feelings, and the heroines hurried at once to the moulding of bullets and to be ready to load the extra rifles that would be rapidly passed to them during the fight. It was shortly after the spring incident, according to both the British and American accounts, and sometime after the demonstration of the scouts, that the real attack upon the station commenced.[41] When

---

41. Bradford says "the Indians rushed up about two hours after the first fire."

the early morning advanced without the departure of the relief force from the station, Girty determined to wait no longer, and commenced operations with an attempt to draw the garrison away from the north-western side of the fort, so as to expose it to a surprise from his main force, which was so admirably situated to quickly overwhelm it. To accomplish this, a squad from the detachment at the bridge site, posing as the only Indians present, made a demonstration on the side of the fort nearest the trace and furthest from the side that was really threatened, Girty expecting the garrison to follow the usual course and mass itself where the firing commenced, and hoping above all things to provoke a pursuit that would leave the station utterly defenceless.

But the crafty foe overacted his part. The watchful pioneers, mindful of the heavy ambuscade so close to the other side, caught at once the meaning of a ruse that betrayed itself in the boldness of so small a party and its evident desire to be pursued. This desire was gratified, but not in the way Girty expected, and not until the garrison had also set a trap, and had arranged itself to the best advantage to meet the emergency.

Then the gate overlooking the trace was opened, and thirteen of the garrison dashed out of the fort, firing as they ran, in an apparently reckless pursuit of the decoy party. But they did not go far—only far enough to draw an effectual fusillade from the Indians between the trace and the bridge site, and then, running back with the greatest possible rapidity, they reached the fort in the very nick of time. The impatient warriors in ambush near the spring had heard the firing, which was to them the signal of the success of their ruse, and, believing that the garrison was fully engaged on the other side, they darted from their hiding places, with Girty at their head, and in a moment of time, as if by magic, an overwhelming force of savages, whooping, half naked, and hideously painted, was rushing up the hillside toward the western gate.

And flaring in their midst was the incendiary torch, a new and totally unexpected danger to the settlers, and one more dreaded by them than all the rifles and *tomahawks* of the dusky horde, for their cabins were as dry as tinder, from the protracted summer heat. The distance to the fort was short, and the Indians were clearing it, with shouts of exultation, when, suddenly, and as unexpectedly as lightning from a clear sky, one volley of rifle shots after another crashed from the port holes of the station into the dusky mass. The Indians were dumfounded and panic-stricken. The triumphant war whoop ended in terrific yells of pain, consternation, and fear.

Confusion reigned. Some wild shots were indeed directed to the fort, and a few daring warriors even reached the stockade and fired some cabins[42] with their torches; but all were caught in the swift stampede as the savages dashed from right to left to avoid another volley from the garrison, and before the echo of the flintlocks had died away along the Elkhorn none but the slain could be seen upon the grassy slope.

But there were no sounds of rejoicing as the savage disappeared, for the fired cabins were burning rapidly and fiercely, and for a few awful moments the station and its inmates seemed doomed to destruction. But deliverance came as by a miracle, for a stiff wind from the east blew the flames and sparks directly away from the station, and though the cabins were quickly reduced to ashes the fort was saved. The siege went on, but the pioneers were greatly encouraged; and not only because they had repulsed the enemy and escaped a conflagration, but because they knew now for a certainty from the long delay of the besiegers and their use of small arms alone, that they had no cannon, that Bryan's was not as completely at the mercy of the savages as Martin's and Ruddle's had been, and that they could at least hope to hold out until the arrival of reinforcements. But, nevertheless, as the leaden hours dragged by, they tortured themselves time and again with the thought that the messengers might be killed or captured after all, and help would come too late.

But the brave messengers were safe. They had galloped at the top of their speed to Lexington only to find, to their dismay, that all its available men, commanded, it is said, by Major Levi Todd, had been decoyed away from the real scene of action, and were pressing toward Hoy's Station, six miles northwest of the present Richmond, which it was supposed the Indians would attempt to capture now that Holder was defeated. The couriers flew after the hurrying volunteers as fast as their heated horses could go, caught up with them at Boone's Station,[43] which stood near the site of Athens, where some settlers on horseback had already assembled, and shouted out their thrilling

---

42. In his *Walketonika* letter or report of August 26, 1782, Caldwell says five cabins were burned. See Haldimand MSS. No report of the expedition from Girty seems to be extant. Savage-like, he troubled himself but little about written statements. 43. Collins' date of the settlement of Boone's Station (1783) is incorrect. The station was in existence at least a year before that time. It was there on the 30th of August, 1782, that Boone wrote his official account of the Battle of the Blue Licks.

news. As Boone happened to be absent at Boonesborough, [44] which was only about five miles away, Captain William Ellis was called to the command of the Boone's Station force, and in a few moments both parties, consisting of sixteen mounted men and thirty footmen, were anxiously and excitedly marching for Bryan's Station.

In the meanwhile the Indians, so badly beaten in an open assault, returned at once to their usual tactics of doing all the damage possible with the least personal exposure, and laboured with persistent energy to pick off the garrison in detail. Rifle balls were poured into the fort from the corn, the hemp, and the cane, from every stump and tree and clump of weeds that could hide an Indian marksman, and the fusillade resulted before the close of the day in the killing of two of the garrison, Atkinson and Mitchell, and in the wounding of the gallant Nicholas Tomlinson, who afterward met with such a tragic fate in Hardin's expedition. [45] But the sharpshooting was not all one way. Jacob Stucker, who was with Boone in 1780 when the famous woodsman pursued the savages who had killed his brother Edward, seems to have had a hand in the fray; for the tale is told that at this stage of the siege little Betsy Johnson ran to her mother with the news that "Jake Stucker has just killed an Indian!"

"Pshaw, " replied the stout-hearted mother, "what's one Indian!" Tradition says that some of the most annoying shots came from a sycamore tree on the north bank of the creek, near where the bridge now is, until a disgusted settler "saw something move" and fired, when an Indian tumbled through the branches and hit the ground to rise no more. Only the big hollow trunk of the tree remains, and it is charred and blackened from the torch of a thoughtless hunter, but it is none the less an interesting relic of the tragic scenes of more than a century ago.

This desultory fighting, which went on for hours, was marked by constant efforts to destroy the station by fire, a weapon that had already proved so nearly fatal to the garrison. As the torch could only be used by openly facing the terrible rifles of the white men, it was abandoned for arrows bound around with the most combustible ma-

---

44. Boone was the leader of the party that went from Boonesborough to the aid of Bryan's Station.

45. This brave messenger, who was wounded twice in the service of the Station, was killed in the fall of 1790 while employed in this expedition as a spy. At the defeat of a detachment of the army under Colonel John Hardin on the Oglaze, the daring Tomlinson, who was in advance, was literally shot to pieces by an ambuscade of more than a thousand Indians. Bradford.

terials at hand, and shot burning and blazing at the fort from close but safe retreats. They fell in showers upon the dry cabin roofs made of clap-boards, which were fastened down with cross-poles, which gave them easy lodgement. Fortunately all the cabins were shed-shaped and all the roofs sloped inwardly, so that the boys of the station who were posted there for the purpose swept off the arrows as fast as they fell, without danger from the bullets of the enemy.

As Girty had failed to capture the fort by surprise, he took measures to prevent its being strengthened by reinforcements, which he knew, by the escape of the two men in the morning, might be expected at any time; and, as the relief party would aim to enter the station by the northeastern gate, the heaviest part of the force was transferred from the camp near the spring to the upper end of the trace leading to Lexington, and placed in ambush on both sides of it. This manoeuvre was executed without the risk of a single shot from the garrison, for the Indians passed around by the creek and were completely screened from observation by the woods and the corn that extended all the way from one point to another. The firing ceased, and the hidden savages waited in silence for their prey.

It was about two o'clock in the afternoon when the hot and tired volunteers came in sight of the station, and then they halted, not only to confer, but in amazement, for there was nothing whatever to indicate the presence of an enemy not a gun was heard, not an Indian was seen, and it was hard for the inexperienced to even believe that the savages had been there at all. But the subtle ways of the enemy were understood by many an anxious-looking pioneer to whom the silence was ominous of evil, and the little force was arrayed for the desperate effort that they knew it would require to reach the fort. It was settled that the few mounted men from both Boone's Station and Lexington were to make a dash together by the trace for the gate that faced it, while the footmen pushed around through a large cornfield on the same side of the trace as the fort.

The advance was ordered and the footmen moved at once, as quickly and as noiselessly as possible through the luxuriant corn. The sixteen mounted men, led by the gallant Ellis,[46] and urging their hors-

46. Captain Ellis seems to have been singularly adapted for this emergency, for he was an experienced Indian fighter, a natural leader of men, and well known to the settlers, especially those from Virginia, many of whom had served with him in the Revolution, or had been with him at Grant's Station, founded the first year of the county's settlement. He had just distinguished himself as the military leader of "The Traveling Church," the most unique and (continued next page)

es to a rate of speed that loaded the heated air with clouds of blinding dust, flew like a whirlwind along the narrow trace. Instantly there was a burst of rifle shots and terrific yells from more than three hundred savages, who poured into the obscured and swiftly moving shapes a crossfire that extended for a hundred yards. That they could ever have emerged from such a gauntlet of death seems incredible, but the fact that they did so is vouched for by an unimpeachable authority, [47] who attributes their escape to "the great dust that was raised by the horses' feet," and says they got safely into the fort without the slightest wound on man or horse. Was the charge of the Kentucky pioneers so much less heroic than the charge of the Light Brigade, simply because it lacked the "pomp and circumstance of war," or failed to engage the genius of a Tennyson?

Cheer after cheer went up from the garrison as the dust-covered squad dashed with steaming horses through the quickly opened gate; but the wild rejoicing suddenly gave way to deep anxiety as the infantry failed to appear and the indications of a violent tumult increased without. Their fears were well grounded, for the footmen, beset by terrible odds, were fighting for their lives. They had rapidly neared the fort unseen by the Indians, and might have reached it but for the generous devotion to their comrades and that precipitate courage which so distinguished the Kentucky pioneers. The moment they heard the storm of rifle shots at the head of the trace, without a thought that such a fire betokened the presence of an overwhelming force, they turned back and rushed to the aid of their friends, only to find that the horsemen had already gained the fort, while they themselves were cut off from it by a surging mass of disappointed savages, who greeted them with yells of fury.

Nothing but the high corn and the fact that the rifles of the Indians had just been discharged saved the heroic band from a massacre quick and complete. The savages, great as was their force, were careful about advancing on loaded guns, with nothing but tomahawks, and the moments that some of them devoted to the use of the powder horn, the pouch, and the ramrod, delayed themselves and others be-

---

remarkable expedition ever made into pioneer Kentucky. He was a native of Spottsylvania County, Virginia, a son of the patriotic Ellis imprisoned by Governor Dunmore in 1775, and descended from a branch of the Ellis family sketched by Bishop Meade in his *Old Churches and Families of Virginia*. He died in 1802 and was buried in the family burying-ground on the farm now known as the R. B. Graves place, on the Winchester pike. See *History of Fayette County*, and *The Travelling Church*.
47. Bradford.

hind them and gave the pioneers a chance to plunge deeper into the corn, through which they dodged and darted in every direction in a desperate effort to confuse and elude the swarming Indians. It was then that John Sharp, one of the Lexington Militia, escaped, for he was too old to have ever saved himself except for the confusion. The wild flight, the deadly pursuit, the yells and cries, the tossing and breaking of the trampled corn, the rapid movements of a multitude of bodies, and the flashing of a multitude of tomahawks, made up a scene that was thrilling but curious, for the sounds of rifle shots were rare while rifles themselves were everywhere. The Indians, uncertain most of the time whether the quickly shifting figures were friends or foes, could use their guns effectively but little, while the footmen hardly dared to fire at all, not only because one loaded gun would, under the circumstances, keep a crowd at bay, but because they would have no time to reload it when it was once discharged.

A notable instance is given in this connection. One of the retreating men, whose name unfortunately is not preserved, was so closely beset by James Girty (brother of Simon), who was leading on a band of the enemy, that he was unwillingly compelled to fire, and his pursuer fell, which brought the savages to a halt, and the settler escaped. But the fallen man, though apparently killed, was soon upon his feet again unharmed, for he had only been thrown by the force of the ball, which had been stopped by a thick piece of leather he had taken from the station tan vat and wrapped around the strap of his powder horn for future use. And so his miserable life was saved. The bewildering turmoil ended with the escape of most of the infantry through the woods and the canebrakes to Lexington, so that the casualties were few. Only two of the gallant footmen were killed, and four wounded, while the damage to the enemy was less still, if any at all.

It was nearly sunset when the chagrined and exasperated savages abandoned the pursuit, and from that time until night they wreaked their vengeance on everything they could lay their hands on. They burned all the outbuildings and fences, damaged the hemp, pulled up the vegetables, cut down the corn, and swept the settlement of its live stock when it returned as usual to the station in the evening. According to the British account, three hundred hogs and one hundred and fifty head of cattle were killed, the few sheep were totally destroyed, and every horse outside the stockade was appropriated. The work of ruin only ended at nightfall, when the camp-fires were lighted and the tired and sullen warriors roasted themselves a supper from the best of the slaughtered stock and prostrate corn.

The Indians were discouraged, their rifles became silent, and a final council of the chiefs and leaders was held. It is worthy of note that Moluntha[48] was there, the veteran *sachem* who was afterward basely murdered by the same McGary whose rashness precipitated the Battle of the Blue Licks, and there also was the infamous Alexander McKee, the Tory, who had hoped that savage conquests would bring back to him his lands[49] on South Elkhorn that had been confiscated and settled on the infant Seminary of Transylvania. The conference was short and gloomy. All agreed that the fort, rude and simple as it was, was impregnable to small arms, and could not be taken by assault; that their failure to seize the place by stratagem early in the morning had given the settlers a whole day in which to scatter the news of the invasion, and the fact that some reinforcements had already arrived was proof enough that the white men would quickly rush to the rescue.

The council favoured an immediate retreat, but Girty, burning to avert, if possible, so signal a collapse of the siege, determined to try first the virtue of diplomacy. Forcing a way through the tall, damaged hemp, he managed to reach a big stump that stood near the site of the present old residence, but which was then a part of the clearing northwest of the station; and thus protected, he hailed the grim and silent fort, announced himself to the beleaguered inmates and asked if they knew him,[50] evidently courting recognition for some

48. Moluntha, the noted Shawanese, and brother-in-law of the great Cornstalk, was the only one of the many Indian chiefs at the siege whose name has come down to us. Four years before this (1778) he was with Du Quesne in the last attack on Boonesborough, and it was there that he accused Boone of killing his son, declaring that he had tracked him to that fort, a charge which Boone emphatically denied. Moluntha participated in the Battle of the Blue Licks, and led his people against Clark in his unpopular and unfortunate Shawanese campaign of 1786, but was forced to surrender. It was while he was then a prisoner that he was brained with an axe by McGary, on the miserable plea that the old warrior had been at the Battle of the Blue Licks. At a court-martial held at Bardstown, March 2, 1787, McGary was found guilty (Volume 4, *Virginia State Papers*), but was never punished.

49. He owned two thousand acres of land on South Elkhorn, surveyed for him by James Douglas, in June, 1774, but he succumbed to British gold, and the land was confiscated by an inquest of escheat—Daniel Boone and John Bowman being on the jury—and devoted to Transylvania Seminary. Fayette County records.

50. Probably no Indian leader of his time was personally known to so many of the Kentucky pioneers as Simon Girty. Kenton was not only his comrade in the Cresap War of 1774, but his life had been saved by Girty four years after that. Clark, Boone, and Harrod all knew him in Virginia, where he was one of Dunmore's scouts; immigrants from Pennsylvania saw him at Fort Pitt (Pittsburgh), (continued next page)

reason from the settlers who had known him either before or since the commencement of the war. He proclaimed himself in the hearing of Caldwell and his Tory rangers as the commander of the besieging force,[51] boasted of the multitude of his warriors, and demanded the surrender of the place.

Further resistance, he said, would seal the fate of the inmates, for he was hourly expecting reinforcements with artillery that would quickly blow the stockade to pieces. He could protect them now, he said, before the extremity was reached, and solemnly assured them that he would do so if they capitulated at once, but he earnestly and impressively declared that if they allowed the place to be taken by storm, as it certainly would be that night on the arrival of his artillery, it would be impossible for him to save them from the Indians, who would then be excited to fury and be entirely beyond his control.

The speech of the White Indian made deeper than ever the depression already felt by the settlers at the repulse of their friends, the destruction of their property, and the knowledge of the desperate straits that even one more day would reduce them to for water and provisions. They doubted the coming of the cannon, and they had no

---

where he was employed as interpreter and otherwise for several years, and up to 1778, and during the four years of the Revolutionary War, between that date and the time of his appearance at Bryan's Station, numbers of Kentucky settlers, who had been captured by the Indians, and had escaped, must have seen him at Old Chillicothe, Upper Sandusky, and Detroit, where he spent much of his time, and where most of the white captives were taken. The prisoners from Ruddle's and Martin's doubtless knew him only too well, for he was conspicuous at their surrender. It is plain from Reynolds' remarks that Girty was personally well known at Bryan's Station. There was no doubt whatever about his identity.

51. That the authority of Caldwell was thus publicly ignored is incontestable. (See Bradford's *Notes.*) Girty was the actual commander, and, however a writer may detest his savagery, the prejudice is puerile and unworthy that causes a historian to deny the truth. Levi Todd, who fought against *The White Indian* in this campaign, knew personally whereof he spoke when he said in his letter of September n, 1782, to Governor Harrison, of Virginia, that "Simon Girty alone had led the enemy during the invasion." (*Virginia State Papers*, volume 3.) Boone, Marshall, and Bradford, who were themselves pioneers, confirm the statement. The writer is, at this date, more than ever convinced of the correctness of this statement, that Girty was the de facto leader, made in his sketch of *The White Indian*, published in the *Magazine of American History* for March, 1886. Even certain recent writers on Girty, either from ignorance or prejudice, are unreliable. One of them, who dogmatically instructs (?) the public, seems to know nothing whatever of Bradford, one of the highest authorities in the case.

confidence whatever in savage promises of protection, but the camp-fires so boldly lighted seemed to proclaim a settled persistence on the part of the enemy, and the dreaded guns might come after all. They would fight to the last, but all the same they shuddered and ceased to speak as they thought of the deeds "too barbarous to relate," as Boone said, that followed the boom of Byrd's artillery at Ruddle's Station.[52] They remembered that Girty was there, and that the trail of the savage force from the Licking to the Ohio was marked by the disfigured corpses of women and children who had been murdered and scalped on the route.

The gloomy silence was suddenly broken by an unexpected incident, especially characteristic of the early Kentucky pioneer. An impulsive young rifleman named Aaron Reynolds, who could boast and swear like Falstaff when the humour seized him, but who soon proved that he was capable, none the less, of gallant deeds, was so wrought up by Girty's speech that he forgot all the restrictions of age and discipline, and, rushing unbidden to a port-hole, he hailed the savage leader and answered him in genuine backwoods style in "words with the bark on."

"We all know you," he scornfully cried. "I have a trifling dog named Simon Girty, because he looks so much like you. Bring on your artillery if you've got any, and be damned to you," he yelled; "and if you or any of your naked rascals get into this place we will thrash you out again with switches we have gathered for that very purpose, for we wouldn't use guns against such as you." He ended his reply with the loud and confident statement that "We, too, are expecting reinforcements, the whole country is marching to us, and if you and your gang of murderers stay here another day we will have your scalps drying in the sun on the roofs of these cabins."

Reynolds did not exactly believe his own brag about switches and

52. It is strange that such a tragedy as that enacted at Ruddle's Station in 1780 should have figured so little in Western annals, and should be so unfamiliar even now. Certainly the settlers at Bryan's never forgot it to their dying day. Some of the women and children were killed and scalped as soon as the fort was taken, and their quivering bodies thrown together in a pile. All the rest of the inmates were seized and scattered indiscriminately, and, bewildered and agonized, and loaded down with plunder looted from their own cabins, were driven off into a captivity which some endured for fourteen years, and from which others never did return. As fast as the women or children became exhausted from the weight of their burdens and the miseries of the march they were *tomahawked*, scalped, and left unburied. (Filson's *Boone*.) Was it surprising that the defenders of Bryan's Station grew suddenly silent as they coupled recollections of Ruddle's with Girty's threat about his artillery?

scalps, but his bold talk served its purpose, for Girty was convinced that the siege was hopeless. He ended the *parley* with baleful expressions of sorrow at the destruction which he declared would certainly overwhelm the station by the rising of another sun, and retired to his camp insulted and incensed to plan the most subtle and successful movement he ever made one which at last drew the settlers away from their wooden strongholds[53] and brought upon them the most terrible defeat they ever experienced on Kentucky soil. Any amount of mere balderdash about Girty was let loose as history nearly a century ago, and much of it has been perpetuated, but in spite of it the fact is plain that the pioneers were not outgeneraled and overwhelmed by a fool, but by a man of more than ordinary military capacity, [54]

That night was the longest and most terrible that Bryan's Station had ever known, and many a fervent prayer went up from its suffering but resolute inmates. They were encircled by enemies, cut off from the world, faint from thirst, grieving for their dead, tortured by alternate doubts and fears about the coming of the artillery, and hoping for a relieving force with that hope deferred that maketh the heart sick. Time and again a volley of rifle shots would cause them to spring to the port holes, but no attack was made, and the alarms served only to remind them of the sleepless vigilance of the savages.

And so, with the dread of the coming of another day, they watched and waited under arms through the interminable hours until their almost despairing eyes saw the dawning of the 17th of August, (see note following), and beheld the sunlight flooding again the beautiful valley of the Elkhorn. They saw the smoke of innumerable camp-fires, but the silence was ominous. Would it be broken by the thunder

---

53. One writer, ignoring the plain object of Girty's retreat, and the fact that he had no cannon, says that he changed his plans because he found that the Lexington fort was "proof against small artillery," a reason strangely irrelevant and not mentioned by any one of the accepted authorities.

54. The war ended too quickly for Girty, closing as it did so soon after the Battle of the Blue Licks, his most important and successful experience as a warrior, and when he was at the height of his popularity and influence among his dusky brethren. One of the melodramatic incidents about Girty, included in the balderdash already alluded to, pictures him as conveniently and appropriately slain by Kentucky troops at the Battle of the Thames, October 5, 1813. One is amused to see such an item accepted in so late a book as *The Winning of the West*, by an author who rejects much of McClung's sketches as "sheer fiction." Girty took no part whatever in the Battle of the Thames, and was not killed anywhere, but died in the same old way, more than five years after the battle, in February, 1818, near Maiden, Canada, as stated by the writer in *The White Indian*.

of artillery? All at once they were startled by a distant shout and the sound of a galloping horse, and in another moment they saw a rider in familiar buckskin excitedly waving his hat. Their hearts leaped into their throats; they tore open the gate, and the messenger with wild delight dashed in, yelling at the top of his voice: "They are gone; the redskins are gone!"

Note:—Some confusion as to the time of the appearance, stay, and retreat of the Indians was occasioned by the departure of McClung, Butler, and Morehead from the dates of the pioneer witnesses on this subject. The writer, therefore, consulted no authorities but such as were living at the time of the siege, and the dates he gives are established by official and other contemporary evidence, some of which was unknown to the authors above named. Such discrepancies as seem to exist among the original authorities mainly arise from a misapprehension of terms, and do not affect the above clearly established dates. A statement of the writer's investigation of the matter may be of interest.

Boone, in his official report of the Battle of the Blue Licks, without stating when the enemy arrived, says: "They attacked on the 16th, and the siege continued from about sunrise until about 10 o'clock the next day." Levi Todd agrees with him and says (Volume 3, *Virginia State Papers*): "They attacked on the 16th and went off on the morning of the 17th." Both of these statements were made only a few days after the siege was abandoned. Two years after this, 1784, Boone, though apparently contradicting himself, really reaffirms what he had said before (Filson's *Boone*), and makes the siege begin on the 15th.

Ellison Williams, a participant in the siege, says the fort was *invested* on the 15th. (*Cist C. Miscellany.*) Marshall says "the enemy *appeared* on the 15th," but errs about the length of the siege.

The latest contribution of evidence is from Caldwell, captain of the Tory rangers. In his letters of August 26, 1782, to Governor Haldimand, of Canada (See Haldimand MSS.), he says he "*surrounded* it (the station) on the 15th, commenced operations before sunrise the next morning (16th), and retreated on the 16th." Bradford, who particularizes with unusual care, reconciles all apparent difficulties in his statement (*Notes on Kentucky*) that the fort was completely surrounded on the night of August 15, 1782, that all the fighting occurred on the 16th, that the main body of the enemy retreated that night, but that the rear guard or party detailed to keep up the pretence of continued siege did not retreat until the morning of the 17th.

We believe Bradford's statement covers the whole ground, and as his authorities are all contemporary, including Boone, Todd, and Caldwell, we accept it as absolutely correct. The date given by the writer in his *History of Lexington* is from McClung, and was accepted when some of the evidence here stated was unknown to him.

The great news, instantly verified by a sight of the deserted camp, electrified the astonished defenders of the station, and gloom gave way to thankfulness and joy, to a turmoil of excitement and happy sounds, and to a half-mad quaffing of fresh, cold water. For a little while they fairly revelled in the intoxication of sudden freedom, for though they had only known imprisonment for one day and a night, dangers, anxieties, and desperation had made the brief period seem a very age. Then there was a quick hunt for Indian "signs," which showed that the enemy had retreated northward along the buffalo trace, after which the hungry settlers made a hasty breakfast, partly from the meat the savages had left on the roasting sticks, and then they proceeded sadly to pay the last simple duties to the gallant four[55] who had died in defence of the fort.

Down past the ruins that the torch and *tomahawk* had made the fallen pioneers were carried and reverently laid to rest under the spreading branches of the forest trees in the little station graveyard across the creek. The disposal of such of the thirty slain Indian warriors as had not been secreted by their comrades was no small task, even with the scant ceremony that was shown them; but they were buried at last, according to tradition, in the bottom at the foot of the hillside on which most of them had fallen in the fatal charge of the early morning, not far from the spot afterward used as the burial place

---

55. Boone gives the loss of the garrison as four killed and three wounded, and the Indian loss thirty killed, wounded uncertain. Marshall follows Boone, and says that of the whites two were killed and four wounded in the cornfield, and two killed and one wounded in the fort making a total of four killed and five wounded, with "loss of the Indians very considerable." Caldwell (Haldimand *Manuscripts*) gives his losses as "five killed and two wounded," a highly improbable statement, without he means Tories only, when the complete exposure of the enemy during the charge on the fort is considered. There is no reason to doubt Boone, who had the respect and confidence of both his own people and the enemy.

for the negroes of the station.

And thus ended one of the most remarkable sieges known in the history of Indian warfare, and so especially notable for the number of strange events in favour of the garrison that were crowded into so short a time that, to use the words of another, "a fatalist would see the hand of destiny in every stage of its progress." The early firing that prevented the march of the riflemen, the wonderful escape of the couriers, the wind that saved the station from the flames, the almost miraculous success of the desperate cavalry charge, and the trifling loss of the apparently doomed footmen, seemed indeed to prove that "fortune fought the battle of the settlers from first to last."

The burial of the dead and the efforts to save as much as possible from the wreck the Indians had wrought were enough of themselves to make Saturday, the 17th, a day of excessive labour and commotion at Bryan's Station, but to all this was added the bustle and excitement occasioned by the arrival of settlers who began at once to gather there for the pursuit of the retreating savages. But that night the worn-out defenders of the battle-scarred fort, relieved from all duties by fresh and willing hands, slept in peace the sleep of exhaustion. The next day, Sunday as it was, the commotion was greater than ever, for one small detachment after another came in from Lexington, Boonesborough,[56] and Harrodsburg, where they had gathered, and from whence they had come as soon as circumstances would permit, and all the morning was consumed in eager preparations for the pursuit. That Sunday afternoon they marched—a little band of one hundred and eighty-two against an overwhelming force—and the heroines of the spring were left to guard the lonely fort.

And then came that fatal 19th of August[57] when, lured by the sub-

---

56. A curious error of Mr. Brown is noted in this connection. He says in an article in *Harper's Magazine* for June, 1887, that "The arrival of Boone and Todd caused Girty to draw off his force and retreat." Reference to Filson's *Boone*, Marshall's *History*, and McBride's *Pioneer Biography* will show that Boone and Todd did not arrive at the station until Girty had been gone a day at least. Enough men to meet such a force as Girty's could not be gathered, and even the most ordinary preparations be made, at a moment's notice.

57. The Battle of the Blue Licks occurred on the 19th, or as Bradford says, "It took place two days after the siege." Joel Collins, in McBride's *Pioneer Biography*, says that he was a boy in the Lexington fort in 1782; that he sat on a fence with other boys and saw the men march from the fort on Sunday morning to reinforce Bryan's Station, and on the next day (Monday) he saw Logan's men pass. As Sunday was the 18th, this not only confirms the date of the battle, but our own statement that the siege ended early on the morning of the 17th.

74

tle Girty, the impetuous hunters rushed into the slaughter-pen made ready at the Blue Licks, and the pride and valour of pioneer Kentucky were crushed as by an avalanche. The horror and the frantic grief that so quickly overwhelmed the stricken settlements came first to Bryan's Station. To this, the nearest outpost to the tragic field, were driven back the bleeding and fainting survivors of the great disaster, and the groans of the wounded and dying that were sheltered in her cabins mingled with the wails of the widows and orphans who were not even to have a farewell look at their beloved dead.

This was the darkest and most critical period in the history of the Kentucky settlements, and for awhile their very existence trembled in the balance, for a return of the savage army in the fall was already dreaded, and if it came with British cannon the settlements would be swept from the face of the earth. Fortunately for the pioneers, they were aroused from a paralyzing apathy of despondency and grief by a trumpet call from the indomitable Clark for a counter movement to make impossible the anticipated invasion, and a few weeks after the Battle of the Blue Licks they were again in motion. With them was a company of mounted men from Bryan's Station, under Captain Robert Johnson, which had joined the quota from the interior of Kentucky as it halted at the station *en route* to the general rendezvous at the mouth of the Licking. The expedition returned from the Ohio country on the 4th of November. Five of the Chillicothe towns, in the region where Girty's army had assembled in August, were burned, the crops destroyed, and the country for miles around made desolate.

But Kentucky's most romantic era was drawing to a close. In a short time, to the inexpressible relief of the crippled settlements, the struggle with Great Britain ended, and though for years after that the torch and the tomahawk of the predatory savage brought ruin to many an isolated cabin, no formidable body of Indians ever again invaded the district, so that the winter that followed the burning of the Chillicothe towns was the last one that saw Bryan's Station with a regular garrison.

In the spring of 1783 most of the men and women of the fort, who had suffered so much together, loaded their pack-horses with their pots and skillets, spinning wheels and "plunder," scant supplies of provisions, seeds, and farming implements, and, with their children, negroes, and hunting dogs, scattered to their own lands in the Bluegrass wilderness. For the rest of the year the fort was occupied by a few of the settlers who had formed part of the garrison, and who from time to time during the summer and fall gave temporary shelter to many a soldier of the disbanded Continental forces who had joined the great stream of land hunters that now began to pour into the Canaan of the West. In 1784 Joseph Rogers, who with a brother had already visited the place in 1782, took possession of his North Elkhorn land, which included Bryan's Station, and his family occupied some of the cabins of the fort.

Religious services seem to have been occasionally conducted in one of the station cabins about this time (1784) by Lewis Craig, who in the year of the siege doubtless preached the first sermon ever heard inside the stockade. A large majority of the early settlers of this part of Fayette County were Baptists, and on Saturday, the 15th of April, 1786, a number of them met at the fort and helped to regularly constitute "The Baptist Church of Jesus Christ" at Bryan's,[58] which has continued to exist from that day to this,(as at time of first publication), and is an inseparable feature of the locality.

The most notable delegates to the meeting alluded to, to organize this church, were Lewis Craig and William Ellis, the leaders of that heroic march[59] of the fall and winter of 1781, which so signally demonstrated that the pioneer Baptists of Kentucky could fight and endure as well as pray. It is an interesting fact that the church at Bryan's had but two pastors in nearly a century, Ambrose Dudley, elected in August, 1786, and his son and successor, Thomas P. Dudley, who died in 1886. The meetings of the Baptists in the cabin on the hill ceased in 1783, when the first regular church building was erected on the present site, across the creek, and it was about that time that the custom began of burying members of the church and neighbours in the churchyard there. The first church edifice was succeeded by another in 1806, and the present, and third one, was built about the year 1867. In

58. See the original church book, still extant and well preserved. The meeting was composed of Lewis Craig and Benjamin Craig, delegates from South Elkhorn; William Cave and Bartlett Collins, from Big Crossing, and William Ellis, Augustine Eastin, Henry Roach, Joseph Rogers, Annie Rogers, Elizabeth Darnaby, Judith Tandy, and Elizabeth Price, from Bryan's Station and neighbourhood. They adopted the Philadelphia Confession of Faith. Before the summer ended the membership was increased by the addition of Ambrose Dudley, Agnes Ellis, William Tomlinson, William E. Waller, Annie Dudley, Sarah Ellis, and John Darnaby. John Mason was first clerk, Augustine Eastin first moderator, and Ambrose Dudley first pastor. Some of the Bryans, Grants, Hunts, Thompsons, Boswells, Monroes, and Richardsons became members after 1786.

59. See *The Travelling Church*, read by the author before the Filson Club, and published in 1891.

early days, when churches were few, the congregation was very large, and in August, 1801, when the "Upper Church," which was afterward known as David's Fork, was constituted, two hundred and ninety-four members were dismissed from the mother church for that purpose.

The year the pioneer church was planted (1786) was also the year of the unfortunate Shawanese campaign of General Clark into the Wabash country, and Lexington riflemen, on their way to join the expedition, saw changes at Bryan's Station. A worm fence partly inclosed the famous hill, several of the log cabins of the fort had been combined into a rude but comfortable farmhouse, and the tall palisades were disappearing, for though the Indians continued to steal and murder, their parties were small, and the strong cabins alone were now the defences in the most settled sections of the district. Some of the old cabins were used as negro quarters, and the place could claim a loom, a horse mill, and a primitive arrangement for breaking hemp.

The trace was wider and enlivened by trains of pack-horses going to and from Lexington, some of which carried out cargoes of skins of wild animals, while others came back loaded with salt from salt camps at the Lower Blue Licks, or with settlers' "traps" and Eastern merchandise from Limestone, now Maysville, to which point they had come by flatboat. The number of "clearings" in the neighbourhood of Bryan's Station showed how rapidly the lands had been taken up, and if the fields did abound with tree stumps that still plainly exhibited the marks of the axe, they also abounded with crops whose enormous yields verified the truth of the reports that had gone abroad of the wonderful fertility of the virgin soil of the Bluegrass Region.[60]

About 1796, or shortly after Wayne's victory, which ended the Indian troubles and encouraged the farmers to improve their dwellings, Mr. Rogers built a one-storey brick house outside of the bounds of the old fort and close to the spot on which Girty had stood when he tried to trick the garrison into surrender. Much of the woodwork is said to have been made from seasoned timbers from old station cabins removed about this time, and it is also asserted that parts of the old cabins were utilized when the negro quarters were built that still remain back of the residence. In the year 1800 a two-storey brick

---

60. The vegetable mould that had accumulated undisturbed for ages made this region a regular hot-bed. J. Morrison, in a letter from Lexington to J. Dodge, of Philadelphia, in 1789, says in referring to the soil: "Grain is raised in such abundance as to stagger belief—one hundred bushels of corn have been gathered from one acre, and eighty bushels often." See American Museum for 1789.

house was added to the one-storey structure, which was undisturbed, and so the building remained until 1830, when it was extended and given more frontage toward the ancient buffalo trace, which is now a turnpike.

No other changes took place up to the death of Mr. Rogers, which occurred in 1834,[61] nor from that time to the present, so that the entire house has remained substantially the same for sixty years, while the original one-storey part of it, which forms the kitchen and "L" of the building, is a century old this year.

And now, one hundred and twenty-two years from the time when the earliest known explorers reached this spot, another chapter, and one of grace and beauty, is added to the eventful story of Bryan's Station. The Lexington Chapter of the Daughters of the American Revolution, descendants of the veterans of 1776, and many of them descendants of the early settlers and heroic defenders of Bryan's Station, have with grateful appreciation and abounding admiration for the immortal Women of the Spring, erected in their honour, and upon the spot they made famous, a memorial which, in its simple and substantial beauty, is a faithful type of the true, the devoted, and the great-hearted heroines of the historic fort.

The Lexington Daughters have been singularly and signally fortunate in this matter, for they commemorate a deed that stands alone, that is without a parallel. Individual instances of heroic women are plentiful, from Judith of Israel to the Maid of Saragossa; from Flora McDonald, of Scotland, to Mrs. Wood and Mrs. Duree, of Kentucky; but as an act of cool and deliberate daring, by women collectively, by a band of women only, by women unaccompanied and unaided in any way by men, the instance now celebrated is unique in the authentic history of the world.

In honouring the Women of the Spring the Lexington Daughters have honoured themselves and their sex; have exemplified their motto, *For Home and Country*; have sounded a note of civilization and inspiration for the better preservation of our historic places, and for the payment of the debts of gratitude we owe to the departed men and women who did so much to make us what we are.

And this memorial, may it continue to designate the spot made glorious by the women of Bryan's Station when the spring it incloses shall have ceased to flow; may it endure while the waters of the beau-

---

61. Mr. Rogers died at the age of ninety-three, and was buried on the place in a walled lot in the old orchard.

tiful Elkhorn make their way to the waters of the picturesque and cas-
tellated Kentucky; may it remain as long as the blue-grass bends and
blows above the graves of the pioneers about it, and be as everlasting as
the hill where the fated Red Men and the indomitable Anglo-Saxons
battled for the possession of a garden of the gods. And, so enduring,
may generations yet to come, mindful of the glorious deed that has
consecrated the spot, stand with uncovered heads before this memorial and still be able to trace this inscription[62] which the gratitude and
patriotism of women have caused to be graven upon its sides:

IN HONOUR OF THE WOMEN OF BRYAN'S STATION,
WHO, ON THE 16TH OF AUGUST, 1782,
FACED A SAVAGE HOST IN AMBUSH,
AND,
WITH A HEROIC COURAGE AND
A SUBLIME SELF-SACRIFICE
THAT WILL REMAIN FOREVER ILLUSTRIOUS,
OBTAINED FROM THIS SPRING
THE WATER THAT MADE POSSIBLE THE
SUCCESSFUL DEFENCE OF THAT STATION.
THIS MEMORIAL WAS ERECTED BY THE
LEXINGTON CHAPTER OF THE DAUGHTERS
OF THE AMERICAN REVOLUTION.
AUGUST 16TH, 1896.

The Women of Ancient Sparta pointed out the Heroic Way—
The Women of Pioneer Kentucky trod it.

---

62. The inscription was composed by this writer at the request of the Lexington
Chapter of the Daughters of the American Revolution, with a view to its use as
a whole, but it was found necessary to divide it to suit the shape of the memorial,
which was done without change. We give it in its original consecutive form.

COLONEL BENNETT H. YOUNG

The Battle of the Blue Licks

A SEQUEL TO THE SIEGE OF BRYANT'S STATION.
BY COLONEL BENNETT H. YOUNG,
MEMBER OF THE FILSON CLUB.

There is nothing more glorious or more heroic in all Kentucky's history than the siege of Bryant's Station, nor is there anything more tragic or more dreadful in that same history than the Battle of the Blue Licks. The one was the sequel to the other. Hardly had the plaudits of the pioneers for the women of Bryant's Station died on the stillness of the sultry August air ere summer breezes carried the story of the awful carnage and destruction at the Battle of the Blue Licks, from the valley of the Licking, by the buffalo traces, to the settlements on the Kentucky River.

The learning, the eloquence, and the scholarship of our distinguished President have placed in attractive and charming narrative the story of Bryant's Station. You have heard with delight his beautiful and thrilling account of the sublime courage of the pioneer Kentucky women on the 16th of August, 1782, and now to me has been assigned the task of giving this club some account of that terrible battle, which so left its impress on Kentucky hearts and homes that a century has not been able to efface it.[1]

---

1. There has been more written about the Battle of the Blue Licks than any other event in Kentucky history. It is impossible to reconcile all the statements in these many accounts. A correct story of this battle has only become possible since 1882. The issue of what is known as *The Calendar of the Virginia State Papers* and the copying for the Canadian Archives the *Haldimand Papers* in the British Museum have unfolded all the facts about this event, parts of which had remained concealed for over one hundred years.

The publication of the third volume of the *Virginia Calendar* was made in 1883. Here first became public the Kentucky contemporaneous accounts of the Battle of the Blue Licks. The papers most important and interesting were: (cont. next page)

Before entering upon the history of the battle it is necessary to deal with a few historical facts and characters, so that you may more fully understand what that battle meant, and what was its cost to the people of Kentucky.

The slain represented one thirteenth of the fighting men in the three counties into which the State was then divided. They were related to nearly all the families within Kentucky's borders, and comprised in an unusual ratio the enterprise, the leadership, and the courage of Kentucky defenders and settlers. The sacrifice that day made was the most costly which on any single occasion war's demand had ever exacted from the infant territory.

It was not so much that they had died. Its commonness had robbed death of its terrors to the Kentucky pioneer. In the seven years immediately preceding this battle nine hundred people had been murdered in their homes or gone down to death in the storm of battle. In this period as many had died by violence as now lived in the State. It was the suddenness of the calamity which gave it so many horrors. It came when every heart was full of pride at the heroic defence of Bryant's Station. When removed from the din and excitement of battle the offering appeared so useless and so reckless, and it did more to excite public fear, to unsettle public confidence, and stimulate public alarm than the dreadful array of all the deaths which had marked all the years since 1775.

In 1782 there were only about a thousand fighting men in the entire State. One hundred and fifty of these were in Fayette County; that is, all of the territory east of the Kentucky River and its middle fork. Five hundred more were in Lincoln County, substantially bounded east and north by the Salt and Kentucky Rivers; and the remainder

Letter of Andrew Steele to Governor Harrison, dated Lexington. Kentucky, August 26, 1782. *Virginia Calendar*, volume 3. Report of Colonel Benjamin Logan to Governor Harrison, dated Lincoln County, August 31, 1782. *Virginia Calendar*, volume 3. Letter of Levi Todd to Governor Harrison, dated Lexington, Kentucky, September 11, 1782, *Virginia Calendar*, volume 3. Report of civil and military officers of Fayette County to Governor Harrison, dated Lexington, Kentucky, September 11, 1782. *Virginia Calendar*, volume 3. Daniel Boone's letter to Governor Harrison, giving an account of the battle, dated Fayette County, Boone's Station. August 30, 1782. *Virginia Calendar*, volume 3. Report of Major William Caldwell, the British Commandant, dated Wakatamiki (now Zanesfield, Logan County, Ohio), August 26, 1782. *Haldimand Manuscripts*, Series B, volume 123. Also report of Captain Alexander McKee, who was in command of the Indians, dated same place, August 28, 1782. *Haldimand Manuscripts*, Series B, volume 123. All these papers are given in full in the appendix to this article.

were in Jefferson County, principally in and around the then town of Louisville. The vast territory comprised within Fayette County had only five forts within its boundary. Savage invasion had caused the remainder to be evacuated, and now only Lexington, McClellan's, Mc-Connell's, Bryant's, and Boone's were left to assert the demands of the whites for the ownership of the land.

General George Rogers Clark was at Louisville; he was the ranking officer in the territory. He had built the fort at the Falls of the Ohio, and constructed a row-boat, on which were a few pieces of artillery. The boat could be pulled up and down the Ohio River by fifty oarsmen, to the point where danger was most imminent.

John Todd was commander in Fayette, Benjamin Logan in Lincoln, and John Floyd in Jefferson County.

There has been quite a difference of opinion as to the exact date upon which Caldwell, McKee, and Elliott, the British officers, accompanied by Simon Girty, George Girty, and the Indian allies, appeared before Bryant's Station. Levi Todd and Daniel Boone both say that the Indians appeared on the morning of the 16th of August. Colonel John Mason Brown has it on the 15th. Alexander McKee, one of the British officers, says they arrived at Bryant's Station on the 18th. Major Caldwell, the British commander, says it was on the morning of the 15th. It is not probable that Caldwell and McKee, in their wilderness campaign, were able to keep very accurate diaries, and a careful calculation backward from the day of battle demonstrates that it was the 16th of August when Caldwell and McKee, piloted by Simon Girty, assailed the place. They had surrounded it during the previous night.

They came like the pestilence that walks in the darkness, unexpected and unseen. They had marched along the buffalo traces or stolen through the forests without having given to any one any notice of their intention. They had crossed the Ohio River at the mouth of the Licking, a place where at this season it was fordable, and in a little over two day's time they had reached Bryant's Station; no spy or scout had brought tidings of the coming storm, and when the morning light dawned on the 16th of August, as the men in the fort were about to emerge from the gates for the purpose of succouring Hoy's Station, the crack of Indian rifles spoke to tell them that they themselves were besieged.

Before the smoke of the first discharge had ascended so as to clear the scene for conflict, two gallant and courageous men had broken through the Indian cordon and, with the swiftness of the wind, carried the story to Lexington that Bryant's Station was in peril.

Colonel John Todd, the county commandant, was in Lincoln County, but Major Levi Todd, his brother, instantly dispatched messengers to all the stations west of Lexington, and called upon the men of Lincoln to come quickly to the rescue of the beleaguered fort. By the night of the 16th the hard riding pioneers had carried the news to Harrodsburg, and a little later to St. Asaph's or Stanford, and when the sun arose on the morning of the 17th the men of Lincoln, under Trigg, Harlan, McBride, and the Bulgers, were well under way toward Lexington in response to the call of their comrades, and when, on Saturday night, the gates at Bryant's Station were closed one hundred and thirty-five of the bravest and most gallant of the men of Lincoln were within its walls ready for consultation and to set out for the punishment of the invaders. With the haste of a rapid courier John Todd had hurried from Lincoln to his own county, and was there now, ready for action as well as for counsel with those who had come to help his people in their dire distress.

One hundred and thirty-five men from Lincoln and forty-seven from Fayette had now assembled. Fully one third of them were officers who in many a combat and on many an expedition had shown their skill and their courage. In those days, cowards did not come to Kentucky. Men who faced the dangers and difficulties of pioneer life were not only heroic, but they were fearless, and of all the band assembled there that night there was not a single officer or soldier whom death could alarm, or who was not ready to face an Indian foe on any call.

White men then in Kentucky were brothers; the peril of one was the peril of all, and none hesitated to rush to the defence of any station or cabin where the savage foe had come; and the camp-fires which Caldwell and his Indians had left kindled had not died out ere the chivalry and comradeship of the pioneers had brought them to the spot where danger and peril were thick on every hand.

The situation was one which called not only for courage but for sagacious counsel. This Saturday night, sultry and warm, and rendered even more so by the wooden inclosure surrounding this little army, was spent in large part in the preparation and consultation for the morrow's work.

A council of war was called, and by the lamps supplied with bear's grease, in the cabins and fort, these soldiers and these officers gathered for the purpose of determining that which was the wisest and best under all circumstances.

The women and children joined in the excitement of the hour, and long after darkness brooded over the fort they mingled with the new comers and told them of the incidents, dangers, and triumphs of the siege. The day and night of this beleaguerment had made heroes of even the tots who clung to their mothers' hands, and the story of the courage and daring of all who had battled within the wooden station was rehearsed with sympathetic hearts and to appreciative ears. The night had well advanced before any had sought repose on the rude beds of the pioneer cabins, or rested themselves within the open square bounded by the palisades.

John Todd, Stephen Trigg, and Daniel Boone were the ranking officers, and around and about them stood men who had spent a full share of their lives in this wilderness, encompassed by the dangers which Indian warfare everywhere introduced, and with an experience which not only rendered them courageous and self-reliant but conscious of superiority as warriors and men.

What a picture for a painter was presented that night! The oldest and best versed of all in Indian warfare was Daniel Boone, who was then about fifty years of age.[2] Thirteen of these years he had hunted and fought in Kentucky. Twice captured by the Indians, thoroughly educated to all their methods and wiles; even then, his record for skill and daring was unequalled by any man in all this country, where every man was skilled and daring. He had already given a brother and a son to die for Kentucky's freedom, and he came with another son in his company, and was ready to go where danger was greatest and foes were thickest.

Loved and respected by all, and chief in command, was John Todd, who, though only thirty years old, had already made a profound impression upon all men with whom he had come in contact. He had been in the great struggle at Point Pleasant in 1774, and endured its baptism of blood; he had ridden beside General Andrew Lewis as his

2. The date of Boone's birth is stated so differently that it is impossible to give his exact age. Collins says he was born in 1731; Flint, 1746; American Biography, 1735; Marshall, 1746. John M. Pick, who visited Boone and gathered biographic facts from his own lips, in his life of him, in the thirteenth volume of the *Spark's Series*, gives his birth in February, 1735. In the genealogical chart of the Boone family, made out by James Boone, the birth of Daniel is given July 14, 1732. Boone himself, while dictating to John Filson, his first biographer, the events of his life, does not seem to have thought the date of his birth of sufficient importance to be recorded, and hence it does not appear in Filson's *History of Kentucky* in 1784.

Adjutant General in the Scioto campaign; he had been a member of Henderson's Legislature at Boonesborough in 1775; he had been one of the men who had risked their lives to go after powder in 1776; he had explored South-western Kentucky as far as Bowling Green in 1775; he had been one of the judges at the first court of quarter sessions in Kentucky in 1775; he had been elected to the House of Burgesses in 1777 and 1780 and 1782; he had been with George Rogers Clark at Kaskaskia and Vincennes in 1778 and 1779; he had been valiant and true and brave in all these years of campaigning, of fighting, of danger, of surveying, and of legislating. He was the most brilliant and best educated man in that distinguished assemblage, and, aside from rank, its recognized leader.

Beside Todd was Stephen Trigg. Only three years before he had come to Kentucky as a member of the Court of Land Commissioners, but when he came he left all behind him; he made Kentucky his home, and he was ready now to give up his life for its defence. With a high degree of intelligence, with a splendid physique, and with a chivalrous bravery, he had become noted for his activity as an Indian fighter, and was now Lieutenant-Colonel of Lincoln County. He had been one of the trustees who laid off Louisville, and had also been elected a member of the House of Burgesses as a representative from Kentucky County. He had been a Justice of Lincoln County; he was a member of a court organized in Harrodsburg in 1781, and no man commanded more of the confidence and admiration of these hardy pioneers than Stephen Trigg.

Close by him stood Silas Harlan. He had emigrated to Kentucky eight years before, and none had been more active in war. He had commanded a company of spies with Clark in the Illinois campaign in 1779. Six feet two inches in height, of magnificent bearing, Clark had said of him that he was one of the bravest and best soldiers that ever fought by his side. In 1778 he had built a stockade on Salt River, seven miles from Harrodsburg; he was one of the men who went with James Harrod for the five hundred pounds of powder which had been brought down the Ohio River for the succour of the pioneers. They started out on the 7th of January, 1777, passing by Georgetown and Blue Licks, and they had been successful in their efforts to transport this most important of all supplies into the Kentucky forts. He had signed the protest of the pioneers against Henderson and Company to the Virginia House of Burgesses in 1775. He came to Kentucky with James Harrod in 1774, and in courage and in experience he had no superior.

Then close by him was Major Levi Todd. While less brilliant and not so well educated as his brother John, he was yet a real soldier. He had settled a station in Jessamine County, not far from Nicholasville, in 1779, and had moved in 1780 to Lexington for safety. He had been captain of the company from Lexington and Bryant's Station in Bowman's expedition in 1779; he had been clerk of the court of sessions at Harrodsburg in 1777, and sheriff of the county. In the absence of his brother he had hurried the messenger forward with tidings of the assault on Bryant's Station. It was his inspiration and noble example that had nerved the seventeen horsemen to break through the Indian lines and enter the fort during the afternoon of the 16th. He himself was on foot, and had been driven back to Lexington, but now he was at Bryant's again to endure all and bear all that awaited his fellow-countrymen and their allies.

McGary and the Bulgers and McBride were there too. They had seen nearly all that was to be seen of the battles in and about Kentucky, and though less known to history they were not wanting in that same high courage which marked the other leaders.

The year 1782 may be justly styled in Kentucky "The Black Letter Year." Only seven years had elapsed since the permanent settlement of the Commonwealth, reckoning permanent settlement from the time when women and children came into its borders, showing that the men who brought them had determined to establish here their domestic shrines. It was hardly two years since the territory had been divided into three counties.

Already the influx of white men into these hunting grounds had alarmed the braver and more enterprising Indians of the Northwest, comprising now Ohio, Indiana, Michigan, and Wisconsin. The Southern Indians, less warlike, in their trading with Henderson had received a golden anodyne, and these looked with but little concern on the peopling of Kentucky with the pale-faced race.

Twenty-two months before Ruddle's and Martin's stations had surrendered to Colonel Bird and his Canadian and Indian army, backed by two pieces of artillery, and Fayette was now to bear the brunt of other Indian invasions. Before the leaves had budded on the trees in 1782 the news of Estill's defeat had sent a gloom and despondency through the souls of all the pioneers, and scarcely had the horrors of this event passed from the minds and hearts of the settlers when Captain Holder's misfortune, in his defeat at the Upper Blue Licks, prepared the public mind for another chapter of woes, and these were to be the forerunners of the most horrible of all that had come into the lives of the struggling settlers.

In the months preceding 1782 a new enemy had come to make incursions into Kentucky, and the name of these Indian warriors soon became a by-word and terror to its inhabitants.[3]

The Wyandot Indians were oftenest discovered making assaults on the Kentucky cabins and forts, and by their courage and cunning and skill and their cruelty they made the terrors of wilderness life more disquieting than ever before.

These Wyandots were a part of the Indians composing the Western Confederacy; they had been known as a fragment of the Six Nations. They had fought the Mohawks in earlier days, and a century and a half before they had lost their prestige temporarily in a great battle fought in canoes on Lake Erie, near Long Point, and had been compelled to move further west. But before the close of the Revolution they had forged their way back eastwardly and had repossessed themselves of their old lands on the Sandusky River. The vicissitudes of one hundred and fifty years of war had thinned their ranks, but had increased and perfected their valour. They had been chosen as the chief nation among the members of the Western Confederacy, as the tribe worthy to have the most distinguished of all honours, the possession of the great *calumet*, the emblem of the co-operation and the pledge of the confederacy. They had this to commend their past prowess and guarantee their future gallantry, and they had demonstrated that this honour was worthily bestowed.

It was the men of this tribe who most loudly called for war on the

3. *Haldimand Papers*. The future historian of this period must draw much of his material from the Canadian archives. The Haldimand collection is invaluable to him who deals with the story of the conflicts in the country west of the Ohio. Sir Frederick Haldimand was a British Lieutenant General. He was born in Neufchatel, Switzerland, in 1718, and died in 1791. He joined the British army in 1754. In 1777 he was made a Lieutenant General, and in 1778 succeeded Sir Guy Carleton as Governor of Canada. He held this office until 1784. He was a severe and arbitrary man. His nephew, or grand nephew, William, bequeathed General Haldimand's Papers to the British Museum. They cover two hundred and thirty-two volumes of manuscript. The papers included in the years from 1778 to 1784 are peculiarly valuable to the Kentucky reader. These papers have been copied for the Canadian archives, and their contents throw much light on the transactions with the British and Indians. It was General Haldimand who permitted and approved the use of the Western and Southern Indians against the settlers in Pennsylvania, Virginia, and Kentucky, and first gave British official sanction to their savage atrocities.

white settlers of Kentucky, and doubtless in the minds of their ablest leaders the dream had been nourished that if the white men could be driven from Kentucky that land would become the possession and the home of the warlike Wyandots, who for so many hundred moons had found no abiding place, and whose wanderings and vicissitudes should at last find a solace and rest in that land of buffalo, cane thicket, and salt springs, which, in obedience to the call of the Great Spirit, produced all that savage life and savage desire could suggest.

Earnest discussion, calm deliberation, thoughtful counsel consumed a large share of that eventful Saturday night, and the small hours of the morning were upon these sturdy warriors before they found opportunity to seek repose for the labours and trials of the morning. The great and all-absorbing question was, should these men now assembled await the coming of Colonel Logan before pursuing the enemy.

All understood that the commandant in Lincoln County had heard the news of the Indian invasion, that messengers were dispatched to every station, calling upon the militia to hasten to St. Asaph's and prepare to march to the relief of their friends in Fayette. It could not be more than a day, they said, until he would come, and with these reinforcements they would be able to cope with any enemy who might invade Kentucky.

Up to this time there had been no very accurate knowledge of the number of men engaged in this incursion. There were supposed to be anywhere from four hundred and fifty to six hundred, but the men who assembled at Bryant's Station that night never calculated danger and never feared Indians, it mattered not how great the disparity in numbers.[4]

4. The Kentucky historians in their statements of participants in the battle put the number of whites and Indians at from four hundred to six hundred and fifty. That they outnumbered the whites even the British commanders in their reports admitted. Caldwell says he crossed the Ohio with three hundred Indians, and that one hundred of them left him the day before the battle. He says nothing of the white troops he had with him. These have always been estimated at sixty. Caldwell exaggerates the number of Kentucky slain, placing it at one hundred and forty-six, and his own loss seven killed and ten wounded. If he thus mistakes the killed it is not unreasonable to believe that he also underestimates the number of his troop. Weighing all the conflicting statements, I put his force at about three hundred—nearly double the number of Kentuckians engaged.

McKee says that the British and Indians were not much superior to the whites in number. He gives the white force at two hundred. He also states that there were upwards of one hundred and fifty Kentucky whites killed.

Some historians have ascribed base motives to Colonels John Todd and Stephen Trigg in arriving at the conclusion to march the following morning in pursuit of the fleeing savages, and charged the fear of Logan's ranking them and thus securing the glory of a victory when the battle should be fought as the reason for haste. No greater injustice was ever done to the memory of brave men. Logan did not outrank Todd. They marched because they were confident they were able to cope with the enemy, notwithstanding his superiority in numbers. They believed that the welfare of the settlements and the future maintenance of the white men in Kentucky depended on prompt and effective punishment of the Indians who had assaulted Bryant's Station; and these patriotic and statesmanlike views brought them to the determination that the best and wisest thing to do was to make a vigorous pursuit at once.

In these the darkest days of Kentucky history, here and there cropped out the jealousies and bickerings which are sure to arise in all human relations.[5]

The promotion of General George Rogers Clark to the position of Brigadier-General in the Continental Army, thus making him the ranking officer in Kentucky, and his efforts to build up Louisville and the Jefferson County forts and strengthen the Ohio River defences, and the drafting of the militia of Fayette and Lincoln to do a part of the work on the Ohio, had caused Logan, Boone, Trigg, and others to feel that too much was being done for Jefferson, and that much of this was at the expense of the safety of the forts in Fayette and Lincoln.[6]

The great military mind which foresaw the benefits of breaking British power in the West, and that planned the Vincennes Campaign and the capture of Lieutenant-Governor Hamilton, and that constantly urged the capture of Detroit, looked deeper into military problems than the militia commanders of Lincoln and Fayette, and with his masterful genius for war decided that the safety of Lincoln, Fayette, and all Kentucky lay in so arranging as to prevent the passage of the Ohio, or in case the passage was made, by a system of scouting to discover the enemy's intentions and route and give timely warning to all large stations so as to make vigorous and safe defences.[7]

In carrying out this, the true and only sure means of defence, General Clark had come into contact with the methods and views of the

5. See Appendix A.
6. See Appendix B.
7. See Appendix C.

Central Kentucky leaders, and already mutterings of dissent and dissatisfaction had begun to cross the mountains and to knock at official doors in Virginia, and when the story of Blue Licks was told, it bore along with its harrowing details a full share of complaint and criticism of General Clark.[8]

The militia of Jefferson could not come to the succour of Lincoln and Fayette, and it was not unnatural that the men of these two counties when drafted and forced to go to the Ohio River's defence, as had been done for two summers past, felt that they were bearing unjust burdens and were forced to do double work for the common defence.

Daniel Boone wrote:

> I trust about five hundred men sent to our assistance immediately, and them to be stationed as our County Lieutenant shall see most necessary, may be the saving of this our part of the country; but if you put them under the direction of General Clark they will be little or no service to our settlement, as he lies one hundred miles west of us and the Indians northeast, and our men are often called to the Falls to guard them.[9]

On this Saturday night, twenty miles away, at the old site of Ruddle's Station in Bourbon County, a far different scene was enacted. Here Caldwell and his Canadian Rangers, with McKee and his Indians by Hinkston Creek, had gone into camp.

The failure to take Bryant's Station, the loss of the men, and the distress of the wounded they were bearing to their own country, filled all hearts with a sense of humiliation. They camped at a spot full of great memories to some of the company. Alexander McKee and Simon Girty had been present two years ago when brave Isaac Ruddle had been forced by Bird's artillery to surrender, and the spot could but awaken a recollection of that dreadful day, when McKee's and Bird's promises to give British protection were so ruthlessly and cruelly broken, and when the Indian thirst for blood had shattered Bird's pledges, and in his very presence the helpless women, children, and wounded had been slain before the eyes of British officers—men who wore the uniform of the most enlightened nation of the world.

As the highest expression of studied cruelty, they had brought with them Nicholas Hart and other prisoners taken at this station, and

8. See Appendix D.
9. See Appendix E.

as they slept amid the wreck and ruins of this once strong fort and loved home, or lay bound by the side of Indians, guarded by a watchful sentinel to prevent even the possibility of escape, they must have had emotions that the human soul can with difficulty even attempt to fathom.

A weird scene passed before their vision, as at nightfall the savage army prepared for its rest. The march of a score of miles since the morning, encumbered with plunder and burdened with the wounded, had fitted all for soundest repose. Meat brought from the slaughtered cattle at Bryant's was broiled, corn taken from its wasted fields was cooked, and the wearied and disappointed savages, after stationing double lines of pickets, laid themselves down to rest.

The four white leaders were not so soon to sleep—a curious *quartette* that now gathered to discuss the future of the campaign, and to map out the plan for the morrow's march.

The commander of all was Major William Caldwell. Born in Ireland, he had drifted to America before the Revolution and made his home in Pennsylvania. He had refused to espouse the cause of the Colonies, and became a refugee loyalist.

He went to Detroit, united his fortunes with England, and enlisted in Butler's Rangers, an organization composed in part of Canadians, but mostly of refugees like himself. He had fought with his Rangers against Colonel Crawford, and received a severe wound, but, recovering, he had organized the forces gathered for the attack on Wheeling, in August, 1782, and, to revive the disappointed hopes of the great Indian army of eleven hundred braves, had undertaken this raid into Kentucky and the siege of Bryant's Station. He hated the American people because they were rebels, and he used his savage allies as a part and parcel of the means required in the war to restore English supremacy over the American Colonies.

By his side sat Alexander McKee, whose hatred of the men of Kentucky was intensified by his treachery and broken parole at Pittsburgh, and quickened by the recollection of the confiscation of two thousand acres of land in 1780, which land had been surveyed for him on the Elkhorn in 1774.

He was a born Pennsylvanian; had been a Justice of the Peace for Westmoreland County in that State in 1771 and 1773; he had kept up a traitorous correspondence with the British, and finally, on March the 28th, 1778, escaped with Matthew Elliott, Simon Girty, and others, to the Indian tribes, and then made his way to General Hamilton at Detroit, where he had been rewarded with a captain's commission, and had been assigned to the work of inciting the savage tribes to make war on the American settlements in Pennsylvania, Virginia, and Kentucky. He was cruel, but he was brave. He had been in charge of the Indians at the capture of Ruddle's and Martin's stations. His soul was black with the recollections of his broken faith to those who trusted him in their hopeless helplessness on the day of that surrender. Now and then a gleam of mercy broke through and over his soul. Here and there he had helped a captive boy or girl, yet he had urged his savages to repeated raids and massacres. He had been at Floyd's disaster in September of the previous year, had fought with his red allies against Crawford three months before at Sandusky, and now had command of the Indians on this incursion into Kentucky.

With these was Matthew Elliott, possibly a little less brutal but none the less brave or enterprising than his two companions in his efforts to murder the white men against whom his British masters ordered him to hurl his savage corps. Ireland mothered him, but he emigrated to Pennsylvania and removed to Fort Pitt as an Indian-trader before 1774. He was captured in 1776 by some Wyandot Indians in Ohio, and carried a prisoner to Detroit, but he had been released and returned with dispatches to Alexander McKee in 1778. He escaped from Pittsburgh with McKee and Girty, and from that hour became an implacable foe of the white men.

His voice with the Indians (over whom his influence extended) was only second to that of McKee, was always for slaughter and rapine. He devoted his life to persuading the savages to make war on his race. He betrayed no trust in his escape to the wilderness when he took up his abode among his brutal allies. Here and there a merciful act cropped out of his long line of destruction. He never hunted the rear in any engagement. He led his red men in battle, and always kept well up to the front in every conflict, and it was only at the Battle of the Fallen Timber, with Wayne, in 1794, twelve years later, that he ever failed to lead where he called upon his Indian troops to go.

Sullen and thoughtful, but not apart, sat another man whose history has run a full course in human infamy. He was then just forty-one years of age, about five feet nine inches in height, with black hair, deep, piercing eyes, short neck, heavy frame, with round, full face, and with a great, deep, hideous scar across his forehead, made there by Brant's sword a year before, but with a frame muscular, strong, and agile, a deep chest which betokened great strength and endurance, and with a countenance which said, "I know not fear nor shame."

A curious life this man had led. He had been born in 1741, in Pennsylvania, on the Susquehanna, near where Harrisburg now stands. His father had been killed by Indians, and he himself had been captured by the Senecas at fifteen years of age, and at this early period of life he had witnessed the torture at the stake of his stepfather by his captors, and he had lived among them until he was twenty-one years of age. He had been a scout and spy for Lord Dunmore. He had been a lieutenant in the American Army, and his company had fought the British in 1777, at Charleston, in the assault on Fort Sullivan. He had been an Indian-trader and interpreter at Fort Pitt for years, and had, at last, under the influence of his present *vis-a-vis*, McKee, deserted the American cause and fled with him to the Indians in March, 1778.

He had led numerous marauds into Kentucky, Virginia, and Pennsylvania. He had given Kenton (an old friend), then a captive prepared for the stake, his life in 1778. In 1779 he learned that a price was on his head, and this turned his heart to hate. He could neither read nor write, but he was shrewd, strong, and brave. He had seen and acquiesced in the cruel massacre of Ruddle's and Martin's stations; he had witnessed the tortures of Colonel William Crawford, and had refused to give him help or give him death, and day in and day out for four years past he had guided his savage confederates to the white man's abode, and with profoundest satisfaction witnessed the murder of women and children and the torture of men of his own colour with a complacency which must have pleased even the devils in hell. He had probably made the traditional speech put in his mouth by white men at Chillicothe, urging an invasion of Kentucky. He had insisted on this incursion into the State, had attempted to persuade the people at Bryant's Station to trust the mercy of himself and associates, and now his soul was filled with chagrin and distress at the unsuccessful termination of the maraud.

This man was Simon Girty, and to him and his three superior officers came now the discussion of the succeeding work of the army of savages who now lay about the cleared space of Ruddle's Station in deepest sleep. Even his cruel soul did not catch a whispering from Fate of the great and complete revenge which would fill his heart and life before two suns again should set. He had no command. England never honoured him with a military office. He was the counsellor and guide of the Wyandot warriors who comprised more than a majority of the Indians now in the detachment, and he inspired their savage action and instigated their most cruel deeds, and on the march and in the camp his soul was busy with schemes for murder and revenge.[10]

When the sun was well up on Sunday morning the Kentucky soldiers were formed in line. They were all mounted. Accounts differ somewhat as to the numbers. Colonel Robert Patterson said one hundred and forty-four; Steele says one hundred and eighty-two; Boone, one hundred and eighty-one, and Logan, one hundred and eighty.

A motley band in many respects was that little army of whites as on that August Sabbath morning it emerged from Bryant's Station, in linsey or buckskin hunting-shirts, buckskin *moccasins*, buckskin breeches, and coonskin caps. The mounts all differed in colour and size; most generally their horses were fourteen and a half or fifteen hands high, pony built, and each man carried his provisions in his haversack or saddle pocket, and every man carried his trusty rifle, his knife, tomahawk, and his patchen pouch and powder-horn, with a full supply of powder and bullets, with here and there a stray gun flint wrapped in a rag or in tow, so as to be fully prepared for any emergency.

The scenes of desolation around the fort were enough to inspire the keenest desire for revenge. Three hundred dead cattle, one hundred and fifty hogs, many sheep, flax, hemp, potatoes, vegetables of all kinds pulled up, a large one-hundred-acre cornfield nearly all cut down, and on every side the touches of savage desolation warmed their hearts and nerved their arms for the coming conflict. Every man pressed more tightly his rifle and his knife, and each felt the impulse of quick and noble hope to wipe out in the red man's blood the wrongs now pictured to the mind of every soldier joining in the pursuit, and each vowed with silent oath to repay in kind the wanton and useless

---

10. The hate of border white people for Simon Girty gave him a prominence in the history of the Indian wars which was undeserved. Brown, Ranck, McClung, Collins, Marshall, and others have made him a greater reputation than he was entitled to. He was never anything but an interpreter. Two years before this battle he had gone to live among the Wyandots by order of the British officers, but he held no commission, like McKee and Elliott, and it was years after the affair at Blue Lick before he acquired any great influence with the Indians.

McKee and Elliott commanded all the Indians on this raid. Simon Girty and his brother George were both along more to interpret and to encourage the Indians than to command them. Simon Girty acquiesced in torture at the stake, and there was no cruelty his word and example would not encourage, but he was ignorant and besotted, and never had either the genius for or the opportunity of command, and the speech at Old Chillicothe against the Long Knives claimed to have been made when this incursion set out is in large measure the creation of the brilliant imagination of early writers of pioneer history. (See Butterfield's *History of the Girtys*).

wreck which abounded everywhere in the fields and cabins about the station.

A few men who were not mounted, or who were not able to make the journey, or who had been told off to protect the fort, stood out in the open space in front of the fort, and these, with the women and children, with hearts full of dread and uncertainty, and yet with cheerful exclamations and tenderest affection, waved *adieu* to these warriors who were now going forth, as they hoped, to punish the savages who had wrought this destruction to their homes and their property.

It was not difficult to find the road on which the departing enemy had marched. They had taken what was known as the middle buffalo trace, leading along near where Paris and Millersburg now stand to the salt springs at Blue Licks. It was easy to follow these roads which the buffalo, the pioneer engineers of the great West, had laid down as best for travel. Once having ascertained the route which the Indians pursued, the marching was rapid. *Vedettes* and the advance guard kept a careful lookout, while the main body pressed on behind, and toward the middle of the afternoon, near the site of Millersburg, on the banks of Hinkston Creek, the Kentucky Army came upon the place where the previous night the camp-fires of the Indians had been built. Here, to the eyes of the experienced Indian fighter, were signs that boded no good to the pursuers.

In many places on the line of the trace the trees close to the road showed the marks of the Indian tomahawk. From the official reports, only within the past few years made known to the public, it was apparent that Caldwell and McKee anticipated pursuit. They knew the spirit and policy of these Kentucky settlers, and they rightly judged that as soon as the soldiers from Lincoln could rush to the help of the men of Fayette an army would march on their trail, and in battle, and, if need be, in death, avenge the depredations of the past week.[11] But those who were pursued were men inured to war's worst horrors. Of late they had drunk deeply of white man's blood and glutted their souls in shameless revenge. The smoke of the fires which burned Crawford and his companions had hardly lifted its hideous pall from the earth, and the blood stains from the successful forays in Virginia and Pennsylvania were not yet washed from their garments.

They had met the white man before and had vanquished him, and they were not afraid to face him again, even in equal combat if the occasion required. There were white men and red men with them

11. See Appendix F.

who had assailed and defeated Estill and Holder, and the recollection of these victories made them careless of the pending conflict which the Kentuckians were anxious now to force.

It would have been impossible to have deceived the men who were following the trail as to what these signs meant, and they had already resolved to punish the foe; and there was no one in all the army of one hundred and eighty-two men who suggested for one single moment the idea of a change in the plans which had been prepared for forcing a battle upon the invaders.

There was something to the Kentucky pioneer dearer than life, and that was his own consciousness as well as his reputation for unflinching courage.

This sight of the camping-ground of the Indians quickened the marching, and a little while after sundown the pioneers rested a brief while and decided upon a plan of battle when the foe should be overtaken, which all now judged could not be many hours delayed. The enemy might be found at any moment, and the method of battle was fully explained to all. Half of the men mounted were to ride hard upon the Indians, and the other half dismounted would follow close behind and attack the savages at short range when their formation should be broken by the dash of the horsemen. All understood and all were ready to carry out the orders. After a brief rest, the command was again given to mount, and near midnight they went into camp hard by the site of the little town of Ellisville in Nicholas County.[12]

All the indications showed that on the morrow they would likely find those for whom they were searching, and none doubted that when the conflict came they would execute prompt vengeance upon those who had killed their comrades and wantonly wasted their property and broken in upon the quietude of their homes.

Since leaving Bryant's Station in the morning they had marched thirty-three miles, which, considering the character of the road and the necessity for caution, as well as scouting, was an extraordinary ride.

They were required to do no cooking. The food which had been prepared by the loving hands of the women at the fort served them for their evening meal. The horses they tied to the limbs of the trees or small saplings. Around these the men slept, while pickets well out in the woods guarded the slumbers of the wearied riflemen. Ere the rays

---

12. See Appendix G.

of the rising sun had lifted their beauteous light above the horizon the camp was aroused and the march renewed.

The enemy in front of them had showed no haste in their journey to their own land. Leaving on the morning of the 17th, they had camped some twenty miles away. During the day of the 18th they had marched about eighteen miles more, and now, on the morning of the 19th, they were only three miles in advance of their pursuers, on the east side of the Licking, at the point where the Maysville and Lexington road now crosses that stream over a suspension bridge.[13]

The red men had not shown any disposition to run away from the fight which the white men were so anxious to bring about. They understood well the courage and impetuosity as well as the promptitude of the white men to punish invasion, and yet they did not avoid a conflict.

The contending armies had slept within four miles of each other neither aware of the other's presence and neither afraid of the other.

Forming in line and riding in the narrow trace, which rarely exceeded seven or eight feet in width, two or three abreast, the pioneers soon struck a little branch, along which the trace wound its way to the bottom of the Licking River. About a mile from the ford the trace left the hillside and turned northwestwardly into this branch and followed it down to the mother stream.

At this point some consultation was held among the officers, and it was here that Boone, whose great experience and whose thorough knowledge of the country gave his opinion much weight, suggested that, instead of following this trace and going down to the river, they should follow the ridge and strike the Licking two miles above, cross at Abnee's or Bedinger's mills, and thus come down to the banks of the Licking some two and a half miles above Blue Licks, and cross the Licking into a wide valley from which, a mile eastwardly, they would gain the ridge along which the trace pursued its way into Fleming and Mason counties.

Boone, with all his woodscraft and his knowledge of Indian ways and Indian life, and with his splendid record as the best of Indian fighters and hunters, backed by the truest courage, had never possessed the quality of impressing himself upon the men with whom he came in contact, or assuming or commanding their leadership. His advice was disregarded.[14]

---

13. See Appendix H.
14. See Appendix I.

The ford of the Licking, from which the Indians were first seen and where the Kentuckians crossed to engage them.

The command "Forward!" rang through the woods and echoed along the hillsides, and down the fateful trace to the Blue Licks ford the cavalcade pursued its march. At the point where the trace strikes the Licking the valley is a quarter of a mile wide. It is two hundred feet on the western side, where the Kentucky pioneers emerged from the forest, and some eight hundred feet wide on the east side, where the foe for hours had been waiting the advance of the pursuers, whose presence by this time was thoroughly known to them.

Men like Caldwell, McKee, and Elliott, and their Indian associates, were not ignorant of who were pursuing them. Spies had been sent back along the trace to reconnoitre, and it is said that an Indian conjurer had, after inquiring of the Great Spirit, told his red brethren that in a few hours the pale faces would be at the river and engage them in battle.

Across the Licking the trace followed up the hillside of the ridge, which was rocky and barren of all trees and vegetation. For ages the buffaloes had come to these licks to find salt. Instinct had taught them the necessity of periodical visitations to these saline springs, where nature had provided this essential for animal life, and for hundreds of years, along these narrow paths, cut out of the woods by the ceaseless trampings of these mighty herds of buffalo, had come millions of these animals to find health and life in the waters which gushed from the Licking bottom. When they had satisfied nature's call for salt, these herds would climb the adjacent hills to lie down and rest through the day and sleep through the night. On those eminences thousands of them would stand and watch the incoming buffaloes as they emerged from the trace on the western side, and, plunging into the waters of the Licking, swim across the stream and slake nature's demand for this necessary product, which here the Great Provider for all animal life had laid up in unlimited quantity.

As the advance guard of the pioneers struck the river and formed in line in the narrow bottom on the west side, they caught sight of a few Indians hurrying to and fro on the bare and rocky hill a mile beyond the stream. Twenty-four hours of marching had now received its reward. The foe for whom they had sought, and for whose presence they had longed, was close by. But the willingness of the Indians to be found, their tardiness of marching, and their efforts to conceal their real number, so apparent to the true woodsman, had caused the wisest men of this command to hesitate about pressing the conflict, when behind them, only a single day's march, were four hundred soldiers

Buffalo trace ascending the bank of the Licking and leading along the ridge to the battlefield

as brave as they, and which, added to their number, would have made them a match for any Indian foe that ever crossed the Ohio River.

The colonels and majors were called in hasty consultation. In the presence of the enemy, renewed caution and the highest wisdom were requisite. As these experienced fighters and gallant soldiers gathered around the commanding officer, Colonel Todd, the difficulties of the situation were quickly discussed. Boone, always cautions, advised delay and suggested, even though now in the presence of the foe, that it would probably be wiser to await the coming of reinforcements before forcing a battle. He had been frequently at the Blue Licks from his earliest coming to the country. He had made salt many a time near to the very spot where they now stood. He had once been captured a little way above on the Licking. With that memory of his, so remarkable as to be able by day or by night to recognize his surroundings in the woods or to locate the meanderings of streams or the situation of mountains years after he had seen them, he told his comrades of the topography of the land just over the hillside from which they had seen the Indians disappear.

Along the neck of the hill the eyes of the pioneers could reach for a mile in unbroken vision; not a single obstruction obscured their sight. When this hill was ascended, the Licking, by a tremendous swing to the north, came close to its side, and from its top down to the river bank led a ravine filled with timber and covered with thickest cane, while five hundred feet across on the other side flowed out a little stream which, passing northwestwardly, ran down into the Licking, one and a half miles below the ford where the army had just crossed. This ravine, too, was thickly wooded.

Boone suggested that at this point they were likely to be met with an ambuscade, and prudence at least suggested that spies should be sent out who should ride along the barren hillside and over to the head of the ravines to find, if possible, the location of the enemy. Two volunteers quickly came forward, and in obedience to the orders of their superior officers they spurred their horses into the river and, following along a narrow bar which formed in the stream, quickly passing over, ascended the bend on the opposite side and then up the hillside. For a mile and a quarter they rode, prospecting carefully on either side, and returned in a little while with the tidings that they had seen no foe. But the foe had seen them.

When they had returned and made their report a new council of war was called, and still it was suggested as to whether it was not part of wisdom to remain encamped on this side of the river where they now stood until Logan and his horsemen, quick and eager, on the march, should come to their help. They knew that before the sun would set Logan would be there.[15]

In the discussion on Saturday night at Bryant's Station, as to whether pursuit was advisable, someone unfortunately had insinuated to Major McGary, who was major of the Lincoln militia, that it might be fear rather than wisdom which suggested the delay until Logan's coming. This sting had gone deeply into his soul. That he was a brave man, those who knew him had never questioned. He is and was a unique character in pioneer history. He had come to Kentucky from North Carolina in 1775, and had known Boone while in that State. He had brought his wife to Kentucky, and she was one of the three white women who first came to the State. He had gone with Clark as a captain to Kaskaskia and Vincennes, and in 1781 he was made major of the militia in Lincoln County. He had helped to build the block-house in Louisville; he had been a Justice of the Peace in Lincoln County, and only a little while before he had, by this same taunt of cowardice, forced some of his comrades to pursue some fleeing Indians in an attack that had been successful, when without loss they had destroyed a large part of the Indian invaders.

In the midst of these conferences, while the soldiers were standing in a circle around their leaders, McGary, always impetuous, and, as was shown by his subsequent declaration, malignant, his spirit burning still

---

15. Bradford in his *Notes* details the colloquy between Colonel Todd and Colonel Boone in the following words: "Colonel Todd addressed Colonel Boone as follows: 'Skilled in Indian warfare and familiar with the ground in the vicinity of this place, we require your opinion on the expediency of attacking the enemy in their present position.' To which Colonel Boone replied: 'I am of the opinion, and indeed fully persuaded, that the enemy exceed us in number fully three hundred; that their main body is at no great distance; and that they are lying in ambush. Their position is equal to an host should we continue our march up the river and be drawn in between the ravines they occupy. I therefore advise that we divide our gallant band, that one half march up the river on this side and cross over at Elk Creek, fall upon the upper side of the ravine, whilst the other half take a position (to co-operate with them) in another quarter. By this means the great advantage of their position will be changed effectually in our favour. But, gentlemen, whatever be your ultimate decision, I caution you against crossing the river at any rate before spies have reconnoitred the ground.'" This conversation is couched in rather too lofty style for Colonel Boone. The use of many words betrays that the language spoken could not have been known to Boone, and that some man of more cultivation and education than he framed the speech.

Place where the Battle of the Blue Licks began by the Indians firing upon the advance guard

under the suggestion that lack of courage had caused his advice for delay at Bryant's Station, and, desiring to vindicate himself in the eyes of his comrades, raised his rifle above his head and spurred his horse into the river, exclaiming, "Delay is dastardly; let all who are not cowards follow me, and I will show them where the Indians are."[16]

From a military standpoint the proper thing to have done with McGary, under the circumstances, was to have shot him dead on the spot. His insubordination, coupled with his rashness and his attempt to assume command of the forces where he was of inferior rank, as richly deserved death as if he had with cowardice run away in the face of the enemy. Yet, in extenuation of Todd and his associates, it must not be forgotten that the men who composed this command were socially equals; one third of them were officers hastily thrown together by the exigencies of the hour and the dangers surrounding the people at the endangered station. They were all ready and willing under any circumstances to fight; they were also full of self-confidence, full of spirit, and each thoroughly conscious, not only of his own courage, but of a wide experience in Indian warfare.

With a foolish pride aroused by the dread that they would be thought afraid to go where any man would lead, a considerable number of the pioneers rushed their horses into the river to follow the reckless and disorderly major, who was now leading the entire force.

In less than a hundred seconds the remainder had made their choice. They yielded their judgment to a foolish taunt, and they plunged into the river, pressing after those who had gone before under the lead of McGary. [17]

The horsemen quickly caught the inspiration and enthusiasm which come to those who enter battle. In a disorganized mass, each striving to find a place alongside the impetuous McGary, they rode across the narrow bottom for a few hundred feet, and then striking the buffalo trace, which led up the hill a little north of the ford, followed it in a northeastwardly direction. Recklessly, courageously, and yet tumultuously hurrying forward, they soon reached the top of the ridge, and then descending for a quarter of a mile they came in sight of the two heavily timbered ravines which, starting a few feet apart on the very top of the ridge, run down north and south to empty their waters in the Licking four miles apart.

When they had reached the slight depression in the ridge, through

---

16. See Appendix J.
17. See Appendix K.

which in later years the Sardis turnpike has been built, they received a few shots from the enemy posted in the timber and underbrush two hundred and fifty feet away.

Through the exertions of the officers some sort of order had been formed out of the military chaos which existed in the little army which had forded the Licking but fifteen minutes before. Boone was thrown to the left and given command. The backbone of the ridge along which the fight was to occur was about four hundred and fifty feet in width. Trigg was ordered to the right, and his route was close to the edge of the ravine which comes up from the bank of the Licking and reaches the top of the hill close to the point where the Sardis turnpike leaves the Lexington and Maysville road. Todd commanded the centre. An advance guard of twenty-five men was ordered forward. These were all Lincoln County men, and they were under the command of Major Silas Harlan, Major Hugh McGary, and Captain William McBride.

Preferring to fight on foot, a majority of those who were not officers now dismounted. It was at once apparent that the enemy in full force was at hand, and that a conflict was immediate and inevitable.

The various positions had not been taken by all the troops before the fire from the Indian rifles quickened, and in less than half a minute a tremendous volley was poured into the advance guard, all but three of whom fell at this first round.

Colonel John Todd, mounted upon his white horse, hurried the centre to the support of the advance guard. They had not reached the spot where Harlan and his comrades had fallen before they were made a target for two hundred rifles. Out in the open, with no protection, the mortality was tremendous, and the crash of this volley had not died, nor the smoke lifted from the surface, when from the ravines on the left and on the right rushed the savage foe.

Protected by the trees and the underbrush, those who had fired had taken deliberate aim, and almost every shot told. Within less than three minutes about forty pioneers lay weltering in their blood.

Outgeneraled, and led by a wily foe into a trap of death, they were not the men to run away under any fire, and they quickly opened upon the advancing and the concealed foes.

The right wing was pushed back by a tremendous onslaught. The Indian line had been extended so as to outflank Trigg and his men, and they yielded to the pressure and recoiled on the left where Boone had made an impression on the Indian right and had driven in their advance line. But when the right, by the overlapping of the Indian left, was pushed toward Boone's rear, then the left wing became unsteady. At this moment it received a galling fire from the enemy, large numbers of whom were soon running back toward the rear of the whites and closing in upon them like a wall of fire. Todd, Trigg, Harlan, Bulger, McBride, and Gordon were dead. One fourth of the Kentuckians had fallen never to rise again, and more than a dozen were already wounded.

It was not often that the men who composed this command had turned their backs to the foe, but it was obvious to the most casual observer that no courage could avail against the men who had made this mad assault, and the merest military tyro could understand that the only chance for safety lay in flight. To remain was madness; to flee gave some slight hope of escape.

The pioneer soldiers had not been trained to fight as organized bodies. Each man had hitherto fought on his own hook, selecting his own tree, and using, in large measure, his own judgment about when it was best to stand together or flee, and no sooner was it thoroughly apprehended that the Indians were rushing to the rear and from both ravines were encircling the whites, than each man by common consent began to look out for himself, and at once the retreat began and immediately became a rout. A few had not dismounted; they rode hard for the ford; only a portion were able to mount the horses toward which they were now running, a few hundred feet in the rear, while nearly half of those who were fleeing were pursued so closely that they had no time even to attempt to mount, but on foot they made their way as rapidly as possible to the ford. Their guns had been emptied at the first fire; the whole action had not lasted much over five minutes; there had been no time to reload, nor did the enemy intend to give them opportunity for any such purpose, but rushed out with tomahawk and scalping-knife, and forced a hand-to-hand encounter.

A new type of Indian had now come to face the pioneers, and he had inaugurated a different and more savage style of war. This was shown at Estill's defeat, at Holder's fight, and at Blue Licks. It required men of the noblest courage to throw away a rifle and rely on a *tomahawk* and scalping-knife, but these red men who were now fighting the Kentucky settlers were men of magnificent physique, and behind this had as nervy hearts as ever entered a human frame.

They reckoned death of little consequence, and they had trained themselves to abandon trees after the first fire and to rush out to meet the foe face to face and end the conflict by personal encounter with *tomahawks*. They deemed this the quickest and the surest way to end a struggle. It was a new sort of experience to the pioneer; he had not then quite adapted himself or accustomed himself to it. The wandering Wyandot, who had been roaming westwardly and now eastwardly for so many years, had schooled himself to this kind of battle, and he had learned that it was less dangerous than to stand behind trees and watch for an opportunity to shoot a foe who was hidden like himself.[18]

The white man, quick to learn, soon prepared himself to meet this new phase of war. The use of the *tomahawk* he could not acquire so as to be on equal terms with the Indian, but the pale-face brought the bayonet to his help and gave its cold steel as a match for the hatchet, and in the future wars the wrongs of Estill and Blue Licks were amply atoned for with the blade now fitted over the muzzle of the rifle.

The unprotected ridge along which the Kentuckians advanced at the battle-ground was four hundred and fifty feet wide. Colonel Todd and his associate commanders had no reserve line. The twenty-five men in the advance guard led by Harlan, McGary, and McBride were scarcely two hundred feet in front of the centre. Taking these from the white force, every man of which was engaged, it left less than one hundred and fifty men in the line of battle. The left wing had thrown out a couple of spies as a skirmish line, but they quickly fell back to Boone's line of battle. This thin line, composed of horsemen and footmen combined, was one third already dead or wounded.

It had been forced in on either side and stood on the ridge helpless, as the Indians on the north and south fired into the fleeing mass now deprived of its leaders and fully realizing that impetuous courage had brought them to almost inevitable disaster.

No discipline could be maintained. A compact body only drew a more galling fire, and organized resistance meant a more certain destruction and increased mortality. A minute's delay would insure

---

18. Colonel Arthur Campbell, in writing to Colonel William Davies, October 3, 1782 (see Volume 3, *Calendar of Virginia State Papers*), says: "The method of arming and arraying our militia ought to be varied. The bayonet and scymetar must be introduced to enable us now to face the Indians."

Colonel William Christian, in writing to Governor Harrison from Montgomery County, Virginia, on September 28, 1782 (see Volume 3, *Calendar of Virginia State Papers*), says: "Even musket men with bayonets would be of more use than is generally thought, as the Indians of late depend more upon the use of their tomahawks and spears than their fire."

the closing of the circle from which escape would be impossible, and which, once effected, would put all the whites within an impassable wall composed of brave savage Indians who would shoot or tomahawk the entire number as quickly as blade and bullet could dispatch them.

To succour the wounded only meant surer death. To remain together was to invite a more deliberate and certain fire; to hesitate meant instantaneous destruction. No order was necessary. No command was required. Officers and men quickly and clearly perceived that separate flight, each for himself, and the crossing of the river, to plunge into the trackless forests on the opposite shore of the Licking, was the only course which offered the slightest possibility of safety. War has horrors no courage or gallantry can avoid. To leave the dead and wounded kindred on the field, to flee away from comrades in a race for life was full of terror for brave men. But battle frequently knows no sentiment, and often hushes and destroys every emotion, and so brother and friend on the ridge parted, each guided by the highest of all instincts, self-preservation, to do that which was best, each for himself. In an instant all by common consent began immediate and swiftest flight.

They had passed over the river a few minutes before one hundred and eighty two strong, full of courage and battle's enthusiasm. They returned now, leaving a large portion of the men and all their leaders but one dead, and the whole force a band of fugitives only bent on seeking escape. They had suffered a fearful and tremendous mortality. Forty-one *per cent* were killed, wounded, and captured; of the captured four were subsequently tortured to death, and this made Kentucky's offering on this fatal day seventy-one of her noblest, bravest, and most heroic sons.

Nothing could exceed the dreadfulness of the conflict on the return to the river. The horsemen rode in fierce madness, communicating their terror to their steeds; while the despairing footmen, wearied by their long run under the burning rays of the August sun, with overpowering fear rushed down the hill in their wild race for life, while the enemy, with delirious thirst for blood already quickened by the fearful slaughter, struck down the fleeing white men with their *tomahawks* and plunged their knives into their backs, and, sometimes tripping them to a fall, drove the blades into their palpitating hearts. The terror was only that which was born of the hopelessness of the situation, and the fright only the fear which came from pursuing the only line of escape.[19]

When the Kentuckians began the retreat it was the first impulse to reach and mount their horses; pursuit, however, became so warm that many abandoned this best chance for flight, for the Indians ran in among them as they endeavoured to spring into the saddle, and a number were killed as they attempted to rise on their steeds.

The deserted horses were taken by the Indians, and on these they rode among the fleeing white men, cutting them down with their tomahawks, or waited to slay them as they ran down the hillside. Others of the Indians rode directly to the river above and below the ford, and then watched for the coming of the doomed fugitives, while still others yet, driving harder, crossed the stream and followed the fleeing pioneers through the forest or hunted them from their hiding places in the thickets.

Boone, deserted by his soldiers, ran forward to find his son mortally wounded. He had only time to lift him upon his back, rush with him into the forest skirting the ravine along which he had fought, and then, bearing him a little way from the scene of the conflict, swam with him across the river and hid him in a cave on the west bank, hoping that by this act of paternal devotion to save his child from impending death. But affection could not stay the crimson tide or stop the flow of his life blood, and beholding the death-damp on his brow, accompanied with the pallor which presages approaching dissolution, his instinct of safety forced him to leave him to die alone. He had done all that love could do to save his son, and without companionship, his soul bowed down with deepest sorrow, he fled into the forest.

Into the river, speeding across the narrow bottom, dashed horsemen and footmen side by side, while down to the very banks the Indians, now rendered more daring by the unopposed pursuit, followed the white men to the brink of the water, *tomahawking* them and scalping them in the presence of their comrades, or shooting them down as they waded or swam the stream.

In this moment of despair and terror and woe two real heroes appeared on the scene. Such men always come at the call of great occasions. Providence, having hitherto hidden its power, responds to the demands of the hour, and men, before obscure and unrecognized, in a moment and without warning rise to the supremest heights and then and there by a single act of courage or heroism win imperishable fame and undying renown.

19. See Appendix L.

Three days before, when Simon Girty had made his speech to the beleaguered people of Bryant's Station, demanding a surrender, Aaron Reynolds climbed upon the ramparts to answer his proposition. Reynolds had not been selected as the orator to answer Girty, but having an abundance of self-confidence, and desiring to exploit himself in the presence of his neighbours and friends, in response to Girty's inquiry if the garrison knew him, said that he (Girty) was very well known; that he himself had a worthless dog which he had given the name of Simon Girty in consequence of his striking resemblance to the man of that name. That if Girty or the naked rascals who were with him found their way into the fort they would disdain to use their guns against them, but would drive them out with switches, a great number of which had been prepared for that purpose; and that if Girty and his band remained any longer their scalps would be found drying upon the roofs of the cabins.

Reynolds had been a member of Colonel Robert Patterson's Company, who had been drawn for service in conjunction with General Clark on the Ohio River some sixty days before. His profanity had disgusted Patterson, who promised Reynolds if he would quit cursing, on reaching the Ohio River he would give him a quart of spirits. At the end of four days Reynolds demanded the promised reward and received it, and from that day on was never heard to swear.

In the retreat Colonel Robert Patterson, who with Boone had commanded the left, was making his way to the river. With a few men around him he was falling back slowly, and attempting to hold the enemy in check so that the fugitives might gain time to cross the river. He struck the stream a hundred yards below the ford savages behind them, the river in front.

Colonel Patterson had been severely wounded in a march to Pittsburgh to secure powder in 1776. He had been fired upon by the Indians, one of his arms broken, and a *tomahawk* driven into his back. He had never entirely recovered from these wounds, and the long run from the battlefield to the river, together with his size, had so told upon him as to render a continuation of his flight impossible. At that moment Aaron Reynolds rode up to Patterson's side, dismounted from his horse, lifted Patterson into the saddle, and then threw himself into the river and swam across, a little later to be captured by Indians who had crossed below and were searching for the whites.

A few moments afterward, left alone with one Indian, he knocked his guard down, ran off into the forest, continued his journey to Bryant's Station, and reached there before Patterson was able to make the trip on horseback. He told the story of what he had done for Patterson, which was discredited and was not received until Patterson himself appeared in the fort and verified his statement. He was presented with two hundred acres of ground by his grateful friend, joined the Baptist Church, and became a most exemplary and useful citizen. The other man of the hour was Benjamin Netherland, and without question he was the true hero of Blue Licks.

Robert Wickliffe, whose second wife was the only daughter of Colonel John Todd, in a political speech at Nicholasville in 1848 said that the majority of the men who escaped from this destructive conflict owed their preservation to Benjamin Netherland, and that he was a fearless man, fruitful in resources, and the impersonation of nobleness and courage. Robert Patterson, writing to Netherland in 1826, says, "I cannot ever forget the part you acted in the Battle of Blue Licks." In Marshall's history it is said of him that he presented a singular phenomenon, and that by his conduct many were saved; and Butler re-echoes Marshall's statement, and accords Netherland the honour of having saved many of the fugitives. McClung, in his *Western Sketches*, says:

A man by the name of Netherland, who had formerly been suspected of cowardice, here displayed a coolness and presence of mind equally noble and unexpected.

Major Benjamin Netherland was born in Powhattan County, Virginia, in 1755. His ancestors were from Holland, and came to Virginia as part of that great Protestant host which settled along the James River in the first half of the eighteenth century. His father was a tobacco planter, and he sent his son Benjamin to Cuba and Martinique to dispose of his crop. While there he heard of the conduct of the British foe in the attack which Sir Peter Parker was making on Charleston. He left his cargo and ran the blockade into Charleston and helped to defend Fort Moultrie against the British assault. In his trips to the West Indies he had become fluent of speech in both French and Spanish. He accompanied Lafayette on his journey from Charleston, in 1777, as far as Mecklenberg County, North Carolina, when that officer was on his way to Philadelphia to tender his services to Washington in defence of American liberty. He stopped at Charlotte, North Carolina, until 1781, when he took part in the Battle of Guilford Court-house, and after this drifted into Kentucky.

In May, 1782, he was at Estill's Station, and was with Estill in the defeat at the hands of the Wyandots. He fought in nearly all the Indian battles from 1781 to 1784. He was with Clark on his expedition in November, 1782. He was also with General Harmar in his defeat, and with General Wayne in his victory, and assisted in the punishment of the very men who had perpetrated the slaughter at Blue Licks. After seven years' absence in Kentucky he returned to North Carolina and married his boyish sweetheart, Theodosia Bramlette, who was the daughter of a distinguished Revolutionary fighter, Colonel Bramlette.

Netherland came to Jessamine County in 1788 with his bride, and settled on a farm five miles east of Nicholasville; in 1791 he moved to where Nicholasville now stands, and built a hotel and called it Mingo Tavern. This house was kept by him for forty years; it was torn down in 1864. I have often seen it when a boy, and I have now a drawing of it in my possession. Netherland was made the first postmaster of Nicholasville in 1801. He was the first Chairman of its Board of Trustees, and his children were the first white people born within its limits. He died in 1838, and was accorded a splendid military funeral. He was buried in his lot in Nicholasville, which is now in the rear of the Northern Methodist Church, and a simple headstone with his name tells where the brave pioneer finds his last rest. His funeral was preached by Bishop Kavanaugh, who was then Presiding Elder of that district. General Leslie Combs, General John McCalla, Major D. B. Price, and Robert Wickliffe were the pall-bearers.[20]

At the Battle of the Blue Licks Netherland was only twenty-seven years old. He was a member of Robert Patterson's Company from Lexington, and being finely mounted he gained the ford in safety and crossed the stream unhurt. As he reached the west bank he looked back over his shoulder, and his soul was stirred with deepest emotion and his heart filled with the grandest courage as he saw his comrades struggling and swimming and plunging into the river or rushing down the bank pursued by their savage enemies with unsheathed knives and uplifted *tomahawks*. He dismounted from his horse, and, throwing the reins over his arm, with loud, sharp, and commanding voice ordered

---

20. Major Netherlands experience in the Battle of the Blue Licks justified him in his subsequent love of horses. He bred a great many fine race horses in his day, and in a letter written by him to General John McCalla, in 1830, now in my possession, he begs him to come to Nicholasville on the following Sunday to dine with him, and promises to show him "the damndest best three colts in the world."

the fleeing horsemen who were thus deserting their comrades to halt, fire upon the Indians, and save those who were still in the stream.

His bravery and his splendid presence, for he was six feet two inches high, restored the spirit of these fear-stricken riders. A dozen or twenty men instantly obeyed his call, and facing about with Netherland, and standing in line, they opened a fatal and deadly fire upon the foremost of the pursuing savages.

The counter attack was so sudden and unexpected that it checked the fierce pursuit of the Indians, and they instantly fell back from the opposite bank. Netherland and his men maintained their position and drove the Indians to cover, while the wearied and almost helpless footmen were enabled to ford or swim the river in safety. Only a few minutes were necessary for those who were in the stream to reach the shore. The footmen quickly left the buffalo trace and disappeared into the thickets, each striving for himself by hidden and circuitous routes to reach some station.

So soon as these distressed, wearied, or wounded footmen were enabled to secrete themselves in the dense forest, large numbers of the Indians were seen crossing both above and below, but Netherland and his comrades, mounting their horses, galloped along the trace and in safety reached Bryant's Station that evening.

The pursuit of the Indians was feeble after crossing the stream. Very few persons were thereafter killed. Scattered through the woods it was with difficulty that the savages could find them, and after a search through a couple of miles they abandoned the search and returned to the battlefield. Here the horrors were to open anew. Those who were wounded were quickly tomahawked and scalped; their dead bodies were mutilated in every possible way that savage cruelty could suggest; that of the manly and courageous Trigg was quartered. From their still warm but lifeless forms every vestige of clothing was removed, and the bodies left where the *tomahawk* or scalping-knife or the bullet had brought the end. Some of the wounded were tied hand and foot, and subjected to a slow death. Four were taken away to the Indian towns to bear the vengeance of their savage foes in the presence of their squaws and children, or were tortured on the battlefield. Three were spared, who returned a year afterward and told the story of their suffering and terror. [21]

---

21. The three prisoners who returned after captivity were Ensign John McMurty (reported killed by Major Todd and others) and Privates Lewis Rose and Jesse Yocum.

On the journey to Kentucky Caldwell, McKee, Elliott, and Girty had, as said before, brought a portion of the men who had been captured at Ruddle's and Martin's Stations in June 1780, and the mind stops still with terror when it realizes what they must have suffered as they witnessed the battle, and then, subsequently, the murder and mutilation of those they had loved and respected, and who had fought with them in the great struggle to win Kentucky for the white man.

Nearly the whole day the Indians roamed over the battle-ground gathering up the guns, equipments, and effects of the dead white men. Here and there one was piled close to another, and their arms entwined, and then in a new outburst of savage brutality new cuts and stabs were inflicted upon the corpses. After gloating over these scenes of death, outrage, and barbarity until in the afternoon, Caldwell marched his forces a few miles toward Maysville and camped, and on the day following (the 20th) crossed the Ohio River.

Colonel Trigg had sent an express to Colonel Logan on the 17th day of August, telling him of the report of the attack on Bryant's, and informing Logan that he and such troops as he could call together had gone to the relief of Fayette stations.

On the morning of the 19th Logan, with the remainder of the Lincoln men, reached Bryant's Station, and toward the middle of the day started to follow along the track which Todd, Boone, Trigg, and their company had gone twenty hours before. They were pushing along the trace a few miles from Bryant's Station near one o'clock in the afternoon, when the advance guard heard the sounds of swiftly-going steeds, and before orders to halt could be given twenty-five Lincoln and Fayette men rode in among them. Their steeds, driven to highest speed, were jaded and fagged, the men themselves, some with bleeding limbs, and all with torn garments and blackened features, told in rapid speech the horrors of the morning's battle, and of the dread havoc at the Blue Licks. In frenzied excitement brother asked for brother, neighbour for neighbour, friend for friend.[22]

The full command coming up, four hundred and seventy comrades formed around the wearied and excited fugitives, as in short and broken sentences the terrible repulse at the Licking was detailed to the rescuers. With blanched cheeks, quickened pulses, and sickened hearts they listened to the story of the awful tragedy, and in subdued and breathless suspense took in the pathetic and harrowing history of the day's dreadful sorrow.

22. See Appendix M.

And now, during the halt, came another and another and still another of the escaping soldiers. With anxious longings and strained vision each of the newcomers peered along the narrow trace, or with acutest tension turned their heads to catch the sound may be of others who had escaped from the calamity.

A strong advance guard was thrown forward, and the main force was halted in the woods on either side of the trace, waiting to see if yet more of the fated company would reach friends and safety. All prepared for battle. None knew but that the bloodthirsty and numerous foe were close behind the whites who had just come in, and none knew how quickly they might be required to meet the same victorious enemy.

Straggler after straggler, riding or running hard for life, pressed within the friendly lines, and each arrival had something worse to tell of the sweeping destruction of the conflict.

Now came one who had seen the brave and brilliant Todd go down in death. Another was close by the superb Trigg as he fell under the fatal fire; and yet another had witnessed the heroic and courageous Harlan sink in the very fore-front of the advance, and yet another had witnessed McBride and John Bulger perish in the leaden storm, while others had borne Edward Bulger away with a mortal wound pouring out his life's blood; and yet others had looked on Kincaid, Gordon, Overtoil, and Lindsay as they too were stricken to earth by the murderous shots. Till near night Logan remained encamped, receiving each escaped comrade with joy as he rushed under the protection of his regiment, and then he turned and retraced his steps to Bryant's Station.

A few of the survivors had gone on with all possible haste to tell the sad story at the station. Of the gallant band who had so grandly defended it, at least one fourth were with Todd and Boone in the Fayette battalion. It was already known now that Lieutenant Barnett Rogers, Ezekiel Field, and James Ledgerwood were dead, and that Jesse Yocum was missing; Jeremiah Craig, whose wife and daughters were among the women who went to the spring for water on the 16th, had gone with Todd, and he had not returned.

The rapidly-riding express emerged from the trace and entered the clearing. His appearance told the story of disaster, and with beating hearts, crushed hopes, and tear-dimmed eyes, the direful story was told again, and each with earnest questioning sought to learn who was safe.

A change had come into the fort. The exultation of the 17th was changed on the 19th into deepest grief and humiliation. No words can paint and few hearts can measure the terror of the scene, and all in silent despair awaited for the tidings from the field of battle.

As the shadows of the night come, darkness only creates new fears and arouses new apprehensions. From out in the stillness and gloom of the forest here and there comes hallooing, and a footman, exhausted, clothes torn to tatters, with limbs all cut and pricked, and with broken spirit and feeble strength calls for aid and recognition. Wives, mothers, children, soldiers, all mingle in common grief, and sit in hushed and earnest expectation, and with hearts lifted to God in prayer for mercy watched through the long and ever-lengthening hours of the night.

This was the sequel to the glorious and splendid defence of the fort a few hours before. There were mothers and wives who, on the 16th, walked fearlessly to the spring to dip water for the besieged garrison, who now in abject hopelessness bewailed the absence of sons and husbands, whose mangled forms they pictured lying on the battlefield or writhing under the tortures of a savage foe.

When daylight came nearly one hundred had arrived. With speedy foot they had run through the cane and timber, guided by the stars, toward a place of refuge, or on horseback, by the traces or circuitous paths, had found the friendly fort once more.

To the experienced woodsman at dawn it was apparent that few more would come, and increasing hours stifled further hope. It was now certain that those who had not come had been victims in the conflict or in the chase. Messengers were sent to neighbouring stations. Boone had found safety in his own fort; Captain Ellis was with him. Some had gone to Lexington, but still nearly eighty were missing, and there were none brave enough to offer to go where the ruin had fallen. At Harrodsburg, Trigg's, and other stations, even deeper desolation was felt. The worst had come to Lincoln; Trigg, Harlan, the Bulgers, McBride, Gordon, were a terrible offering for that county to pay for the common defence. The cries of the widows and orphans and the sobs of mothers went up from every station in Fayette and half of those in Lincoln, and gloom, distrust, and disquietude brooded over the whole territory.

During the 20th, 21st, 22nd, 23rd, and part of the 24th Logan and his command remained at Bryant's.

The spirit of the bravest men seemed cowed. The blow the savages had given was so tremendous and so stunning that none seemed to recover from its force. Andrew Steele [23] in his quaint words told the story thus:

> To express the feelings of the inhabitants of both the Counties at this Rueful scene of unparalleled Barbarities barre all words and cuts Description short.

With the list of honoured and brave dead and the roll of those hitherto invincible recoiling before the Indians, it seemed unwise again to face such an enemy, and the stoutest hearts hesitated before again grappling with such foes.

The friends of the dead both in Lincoln and Fayette were now clamouring for news from the battlefield, and on the 24th Colonel Logan, with five hundred men, began the march for the Licking. On the morning of the 25th they commenced the descent into the valley. Long before they caught sight of the hills on the eastern bank, where here and there vision broke through the dense shade of the trace, they saw high in the air great troops of winged scavengers swarming and sailing over the battle-ground, and these told in unmistakable signs of the shocking sights soon to greet their eyes.

In the river, in the valley, on the hillside, on the ridge, it was the same terrible, harrowing sight of savage desecration. Brothers, relations, and friends began the eager search of mutilated forms, but only in a few instances could identity be established. A common grave on the field where they had died was decreed them, and within a few feet of where Todd, Trigg, Harlan, and McBride had fallen, on the side of the ridge where the left wing had felt the shock of the fierce storm and the quick assault with the blade, the thin earth was scraped away. A stone wall, forty feet in length and four feet high, was built, and in behind this the bodies of the gallant slain were sepulchred; over them were thrown rocks, logs, and brush, and the story of the Blue Licks was closed. [24]

Logan marched back to Bryant's Station, reaching there the 26th, and on the day before Caldwell and McKee had reached Wakatamiki, now Zanesfield, Logan County, Ohio, one hundred and forty-two miles distant, and from there reported to their British masters of their bloody work.

In short season after the battle the buffaloes, driven farther west by the presence of the white men, ceased their coming to the springs

---

23. See Appendix N.
24. See Appendix O.

to which they had so long journeyed. Nature, sympathizing with the sadness and glory which centred around this treeless eminence, exerted its forces to hide the nakedness and ruin and clothe the sterile area with beautiful evergreens. It bade the cedar with its never-dying leaves and unchanging verdure to spring from the rocky soil and stand as a monument to the noble heroes who rest in death beneath its protecting shades in unknown and unmarked graves. Over the once barren hillside this beautiful tree has grown in such luxuriant abundance as to cover every rock and crag with its perennial freshness, and those who approach it now look only upon a mountain of never-fading green; fit emblem of the memory of the brave, chivalrous, and gallant men who here died for Kentucky.

Appendix

APPENDIX A.

Officers of Fayette County, Kentucky, to Governor Harrison, of Virginia.

(*Virginia Calendar,* Volume 3)

Lexington, Fayette Co. Septem 11th, 1782.
Sir: The officers, civil as well as military, of this county, beg the attention of your Excellency and the honourable council. The number of the enemy that lately penetrated into our county, their behavior; adding to this our late unhappy defeat at the Blue Licks, fill us with the greatest concern and anxiety. The loss of our worthy officers and souldiers who fell there the 19th of August, we sensibly feel and deem our situation truly alarming. We can scarcely behold a spot of earth, but what reminds us of the fall of some fellow adventurer massacred by savage hands. Our number of militia decreases.

Our widows and orphans are numerous, our officers and worthiest men fall a sacrifice. In short sir, our settlement, hitherto formed at the expense of treasure and much blood seems to decline, and if something is not speedily done, we doubt will wholly be depopulated.

The executive we believe think often of us and wish to protect us, but Sir, we believe any military operations that for 18 months have been carried on in consequence of orders from the executive, have rather been detrimental than beneficial. Our Militia are called on to do duty in a manner that has a tendency to protect Jefferson County, or rather Louisville, a town without inhabitants, a fort situated in such a manner, that the enemy coming with a design to lay waste our country, would scarcely come within one hundred miles of it, and our own frontiers open and unguarded.

Our inhabitants are discouraged, 'tis now near two years since the division of the county and no surveyor has ever appeared among us, but has by appointment from time to time deceived us. our principal expectations of strength are from him. during his absence from the county claimants of land disappear, when if otherwise, they would be an additional strength.

We entreat the executive to examine into the cause, and remove it speedily. If it is thought impracticable to carry the war into the enemy's country, we beg the plan of building a garrison at the mouth of Limestone and another at the mouth of Licking, formerly prescribed by your Excellency, might be again adopted and performed. A garrison at the mouth of Limestone, would be a landing place for adventurers from the back parts of Pensylvania and Virginia, adjacent to a large body of good land which would be speedily settled would be in the enemy's principal crossing place, not more than fifty miles from Lexington our largest settlement, and might readily be furnished with provision from above, till they would be supplied from our settlements here.

Major Netherland, we expect will deliver this, he will attend to give any particular information that may be deemed necessary. Humanity towards inhabitants destitute of hopes of any other aid, will surely induce your Excellency to spare from the interior parts of the state 200 men, and a few pieces of artillery for those purposes above mentioned.

We are Sir, your Excellency's most obedient and very Honourable Servants

> Daniel Boone.
> Levi Todd.
> R. J. Patterson.
> B. Netherland.
> Eli Cleveland.
> Wm. Henderson.
> Wm. Mcconnall.
> John Craig.
> Wm. Mcconnell.

Appendix B.

G. R. Clark To Governor Harrison.
(*Virginia Calendar,* Volume 3)

Cove Spring, Lincoln County, October 18, 1782. Sir: Yours by Maj. Walls came safe to hand the 30th July. Nothing could be more timely than the cloathing, for desertion was so common, that I believe in a month more there would not have been a soldier left. The works at the Falls was forwarded by every means in our power, until they were supposed sufficiently strong to withstand any attack from their enemy but not yet compleat.

Those preparations that were made and the measure taken to let the enemy know that we were fully acquainted with their design (which in fact we were) I believe has saved the Western Country, by their losing all hopes of reducing the falls, divided their force, sent some to Weeling, and the main body to make a diversion on Fayette County. And had it not have been for that imprudent affair at the Blue Licks, the country would have sustained very little damage. I learn Col: Logan has sent you a full account of the whole transaction. The conduct of those unfortunate gents was extremely reprehensible. The enemy continue to sculk in small parties in different parts of the country but do little damage at present. The movements of the enemy last spring and summer put it entirely out of our power to establish the posts at the mouth of Kentucky, Licking, &c. , they may be begun this fall.

★★★★★★

A late stroke of your Excellency hath added greatly to the strength of this country, That of ordering the delinquents of the counties to do duty with the regular troops in this quarter; it will have most salutary effects although few examples may be made. . . . The works at the falls was at the expense of a considerable quantity of flour, as were obliged to make a fund of it. The gallee I had built answered the design exceedingly, and hath been of infinite service. Our circumstances would not admit of her being as compleat as I could have wished, but I hope to have her so this fall. I have discovered that open small boats will by no means answer the purpose of cruising on the river as they are often liable to be ambuscaded when they came near the shore, or in narrow parts of the river. But those on the construction of the gallee, where gunnils are four feet bullet proof with false gunnils that play on strong hinges, Raise her sides so high that she can lay within pistol shot of the shore without the least danger.

I have the honour to be Dear Sir, your Excellency's Devoted and very humble Servant, &c. &c.

APPENDIX C.

Colonel S. Clark to Governor Harrison.

(Virginia Calendar, Volume 3)

Lincoln, Ky., November 30, 1782.

Colo. Todd's militia was excused from all other duty but that of keeping out proper scouts and spies on the Ohio and elsewhare to discover the approach of the enemy, to give time and to imbody a sufficient force to repell them, as it could not be previously done, not certainly knowing in what quarter they would make their stroke instead of those necessary duties being done in which their salvation apparently depended, the enimy was suffered to penetrate deliberately into the bowels of their country and make the attack before they ware discovered, this I believe is what is wished to be blinded, and the neglect to be one of the principal springs to that mad pursuit and carnage of the Blue Licks, as the reverse of fortune would have obliviated the former neglect.

I must confess that I have been defitient in my duty in not given you an account of every circumstance attending this unhappy affair, but hope to be excused as it was only owing to my delicacy in affecting the memory of the gentlemen who fell, not conceiving it to be of singular advantage to government, and knowing it would fix an eternal stigmy on others characters, but as the scale has turned to the amazement of many, I shall immediately collect every circumstance relative to the whole affair for you perutial. . . . (He begs the governor not to listen to further complaints, and feels persuaded that if he knew). . . the true character of many of these gentlemen (that he would never refer to them again. Gives as apology for this remark, the zeal he has for the public interest, and the estimate he has of his goodness. Referring again to the memorial from Fayette County, he adds, it was). . .to cover their misconduct, and a prelude to a Majors Commission for a triffle and a Col's for a person something more deserving, to the prejudice of a valuable man Mr. Swearingin, their former major who had been absent for some time and was dayly expected, which would have prevented their design, to my certain knowledge they now dread the Execution of what a few of them were deluded to pray for again, Col: Donoldson, who was last spring chairman of the committee that endeavored to subvert the government and cost us soe much trouble to overset, since bearing an important commission, &c.

Appendix D.

Andrew Steele to the Governor of Virginia.
(*Virginia Calendar,* Volume 3.)
Fayette County, Kentucky, Lexington, Septem 12th, 1782.
Sir: The present Important and allarming crisis claim the serious attention and mature deliberation of Your Excellency and the Honourable House. The frequent incursions and hostile depredations of a savage enemy upon our exterior posts, our dispersed legions, our veteran army defeated, our widows tears and orphans cries grate strongly on the ear, nay thunder at the door of your council, not only for acts of consideration, but protection and redress.

To express the feelings of the inhabitants at the ruefull scenes of barbarities daily perpetrated amongst us, barrs all words and cut description short. So fatal is the stroke that a second similar to that we have already received will close the catastrophy and terminate the intire devastation of our county. I would beg leave to inform you that annually since the seventeen hundred and seventy-eight, an army of not less than three hundred saveges infested our territories and since seventy-six, eight hundred and sixty effective men fell, the matchless massacread victims of their unprecendented cruelty.

A few of the primitive adventurers yet survive, who supplicate your excellencies immediate interposition in their behalf, in granting them such strength, as may enable them to carry on an offensive war, or at least act in the defensive with safety, for if some mode of preservation is not speedily adopted the welthy will forthwith emigrate to the interior parts of the settlement and the poor to the Spaniards. Dreadful alternative!! Nature recoils at the thought! further, from the jealous apprehension of the inhabitants I am under the disagreeable necessity of informing your Excellency that from the detainour of our county surveyor (from whom their greatest expectations of strength was derived) they are induced to believe you have either withdrawn that paternal care which they have long relyed on or rather the executive body are dubious of the authenticity of their claim to those western territories.

I would also observe that the many military operations hitherto effected, or rather intended for our safety (the seventeen hundred and eighty Indian expedition excluded, the honour whereof is justly due to the militia) have centered at Louisville, a town distant one hundred miles from the center of our county, to which together with Fort Jefferson, Elinois and St. Vincennes, may the innormous expence of the western frontiers be attributed and not to the counties of Kanetucky, which in competition would be less than a mathematical point.

To conclude, permit us, once more the indigent offspring of an oppulent father, if not equally to share, yet to partake of your kind patronage and protection and beg you would adopt such measures as your superior wisdom mey suggest to promote the peace, welfare and tranquility of your suppliants in particular and the interest of the commonwealth in general.

Then shall we congratulate ourselves in having you the illustrious patron and protector of our lives, laws and religious liberties, when the annals of history will rank your name among the bravest and wisest politicians and gratitude like a torrent will flow from the heart of every Kanetuckian, whilst we experience with what firmness you have supported our interest. Our universal joy and fervent expressions of allegiance and gratitude.

These public testimonials of our felicities will be too convincing proofs to require any argument to support them.

The Author begs leave to subscribe himself a friend to the Commonwealth and your Excellency's most obedient humble Servant.

Appendix E

Extract From Boone's Letter to Governor Harrison
(*Calendar of Virginia State Papers*, Volume 3)

See also report of Logan.

> I am inclined to believe that when Your Excellency and Council become acquainted with the military operations in this country, that you will not think them so properly conducted as to answer the general interests of Kentucky. From the accounts we had received by prisoners, who had escaped this Spring, we were confident of an invasion from the Detroit Indians. Common safety then made some scheme of defence necessary for which purpose I was called upon by General Clark to attend a council, and after consulting matters it was determined to build a fort at the mouth of Licking, and shortly I received his order for one hundred men to attend this business with a certain number from Fayette. Before the day of rendezvous, I was instructed to send the men to the Falls of the Ohio in order to build a strong garrison and a row galley, thus by weakening one end to strengthen another, the upper part of the country was left exposed and the enemy, intercepting our designs, brought their intended expedition against the frontiers of Fayette.

See also address of Civil and Military Officers of Fayette County:

> The executives, we believe, think often of us and wish to protect us. But sir, we believe any military operations that for eighteen months have been carried on in consequence of orders from the executive, have rather been detrimental than beneficial. Our militia are called on to do duty in a manner that has a tendency to protect Jefferson County, or rather, Louisville, a town without inhabitants, a fort situtated in such a manner that the enemy, coming with the design to lay waste our country, will scarcely come within one hundred miles of it, and our own frontiers open and unguarded.

Nor was General Clark slow to express his dissatisfaction of the conduct of the officers in charge at Blue Licks. He thought the sacrifice the result of imprudence and recklessness, and he hastened to inform the Governor of Virginia that the responsibility in the matter was none of his.

See also letter of General Clark to Governor Harrison, dated Cove Spring, Lincoln County, October 18, 1782:

> Had it not been for that imprudent affair at the Blue Licks the country would have sustained very little damage. I learn Colonel Logan has sent you a full account of the whole transaction. The conduct of these unfortunate gents was extremely reprehensible. The enemy continued to skulk in small parties in different parts of the country, but do little damage at present.

See also letter, Clark to Governor Harrison, dated Lincoln County, November 30, 1782:

> Colonel Todd's militia was excused from all other duty but that of keeping out proper scouts and spies on the Ohio and elsewhere to discover the approach of the enemy, to give time and to embody a sufficient force to repel them, as it could not be previously done, not certainly knowing in what quarter they would make their stroke. Instead of those necessary duties being done, in which their salvation apparently depended, the enemy was suffered to penetrate deliberately into the bowels of their country and make the attack before they were discovered. This, I believe, is what is wished to be blinded and the neglect to be one of the principal springs to that mad pursuit and carnage of the Blue Licks, as the reverse of fortune would have obliviated the former neglect.

Appendix F.

Extract of a Letter from Captain Caldwell, Dated at Wakitamiki, August 26, 1782.

(*Haldimand Papers*, Series B, Volume 123.)

When I last had the pleasure of writing you I expected to have struck at Wheeling as I was on my march for that place, but was overtaken by a messenger from the Shawnese who informed me the enemy was on their march for their country which obliged me to turn their way, and to my great mortification found the alarm false and that it was owing to a gondals coming up to the mouth of Licking Creek and landing some men upon the South side of the Ohio which when the Indians saw supposed it must be Clark. It would have been a lucky circumstance if they had come on as I had eleven hundred Indians on the ground and three hundred within a days march of me.

When the report was contradicted they mostly left us. Many of them had left their towns no ways equipped for war, as they expected as well as myself to fight in a few days; notwithstanding I was determined to pay the enemy a visit with as many Indians as would follow me: accordingly I crossed the Ohio with three hundred Indians and rangers and marched for Bryants Station, Kentuck, and surrounded the fort the 15th in the morning, and tried to draw 'em out by sending up a small party to try to take a prisoner and shew themselves, but the Indians were in too great a hurry and the whole shewed too soon. I then saw it was in vain to wait any longer and so drew nigh the fort, burnt 3 houses which are part of the fort but the wind being contrary prevented it having the desired effect. Killed upwards of 300 hogs, 150 head of cattle and a number of sheep, took a number of horses, pulled up and destroyed their potatoes, cut down a great deal of their corn, burnt their hemp and did other considerable damage. By the Indians exposing themselves too much we had 5 killed and 2 wounded.

We retreated the 16th, and came as far as Riddle's former station, when nigh 100 Indians left me as they went after their things they left at the Forks of Licking and I took the road by the Blue Licks as it was nigher and the ground more advantageous in case the enemy should pursue us, got to the Licks on the 17th and encamped.

On the 18th, in the morning one of my party that was watching the road came in and told me the enemy was within a mile of us, upon which I drew up to fight them. At half past seven they advanced in three divisions in good order, they had spied some of us and it was the very place they expected to overtake us. We had but fired one gun till they gave us a volley and stood to it very well for some time, till we rushed in upon them, when they broke immediately. We pursued for about two miles, and as the enemy was mostly on horseback, it was in vain to follow further.

We killed and took one hundred and forty six. Amongst the killed is Col. Todd the Commander, Col. Boon, Lt. Col. Trigg, Major Harlin who commanded their infantry, Major Magara and a number more of their officers. Our loss is Monsr. LaBute killed; he died like a warrior fighting arm to arm, six Indians killed and ten wounded. The Indians behaved extremely well and no people could behave better than both officers and men in general. The Indians I had with me were the Wyandots and Lake Indians. The Wyandots furnished me with what provision I wanted, and behaved extremely well.

Endorsed:—entered in book marked B No. 3 extract of a letter from Capt. Caldwell to Major De Peyster, dated at Wakitamiki Aug. 26th, 1782.

Appendix G

Colonel Levi Todd to Governor Harrison and Council
(*Virginia Calendar,* Volume 3)
Lexington, Fayette County, Kentucky, September 11th, 1782.

Sir: Enclosed is a copy of the recommendations made at our last court; so great a change proceeds from a cause truly lamentable, the loss of our county lieutenants, and a number of subaltans at the late attacks, but particularly at our defeat at the Blue Licks when the enemy put us wholly to the rout the circumstances and particulars are these On the 16th of August a party of Indians appeared at Bryants and by their behavoir a large party was supposed to lie around the fort. An express was sent here, my brother being absent, I went with about 30 men discovery and force my way into the fort, near Bryants I was joined with about 10 more, finding the enemy lay round, we attempted forcing our way. 17 men on horseback rushed in, the greater part of rest being on foot were prevented and overpowered, obliged to seek safety by flight with the loss of one killed and 3 wounded, one of which died the next morning—I immediately despatched an express to Col: Trigg the highest officer in Lincoln, demanding assistance, and also notice to Colo. Jno. Todd then in Lincoln.

The enemy commanded by Simon Girty made an attempt to fire the fort, but were prevented with much loss. They however kept up a smart fire till the morning of the 17th when they went off—the same evening Col: Jno: Todd and Colo. Trigg arrived with a party of men, who with what we could raise soon made 170. On the morning of the 18th we pursued on their trail. On the morning of the 19th we came within sight of the enemy about ¾ of a mile, north of the Lower Blue Licks—we dismounted and began the attack with vigour, from our left the enemy retreated and we gained ground. Our right within a minute or two gave way and found themselves to be flanked by the enemy. Our line then gradually gave way from our right to our left till the whole broke in confusion. The action lasted about five minutes.

Our loss as near as we can ascertain is sixty-six, among whom were our commanding officer Col: John Todd, Col: Trigg, Capts: Gordon, McBride, Kinkaid and Overton, Major Harlan, Major Bulger (who since died of his wounds) Mr. Jos: Lindsay and several gentlemen of note—the enemy we suppose consisted of three or four hundred—they took some prisoners, we suppose though very few, upwards of 40 were found, but we think a number more lay near the battle ground. The enemy must have suffered considerably, a great part of our men fought with much resolution and activity. The conduct of the officers is by some censured and charged with want of prudence in attacking at any rate, but as we had no chance to know their number, we thought ours was not much inferior and supposed we should by a fierce attack throw them in confusion and break their lines. We are much alarmed in this county and fear the consequence will be very detrimental if government cannot give assistance, though our great dependence is that if the county surveyor would attend, we should be strengthened with additional settlers not a few.

I am Sir, Your Excellency's most obedient and very Humble servant &c. &c.

Appendix H.
From Canadian Archives—Colonial Office Records.
Series 2, Volume 20

Sir: My letter of the 22nd. and 23rd. of July informed you of the reports brought us of the enemy's motions at that time which was delivered by the chiefs of the Standing Stone Village and confirmed by belts and strings of *wampum* in so earnest a manner that could not but gain credit with us. We had upon this occasion the greatest body of Indians collected to an advantageous piece of ground near the Priowee Village that have been assembled in this quarter since the commencement of the war and perhaps may never be in higher spirits to engage the enemy when the return of scouts from the Ohio informed us that the accounts we had received was false. This disappointment notwithstanding all our endeavours to keep them together occasioned them to disperse in disgust with each other; the inhabitants of the country who were the most immediately interested in keeping in a body were the first that broke off and though we advanced towards the Ohio with upwards of three hundred Hurons and Lake Indians, few of Delawares, Shawnese or Mingoes followed us.

On our arrival at the Ohio we remained still in uncertainty with respect to the enemy's motions, and it was thought best from hence to send scouts to the Falls, and that the main body should advance into the enemy's country and endeavour to lead out a party from some of their forts by which we might be able to gain some certain intelligence; accordingly we crossed the Ohio and arrived the 18th. inst. at one of the enemy's settlements called Bryan's Station, but the Indians discovered their numbers prevented their coming out and the Lake Indians finding this rushed up to the fort and set several out houses on fire but at too great a distance to touch the fort, the wind blowing the contrary way.

The firing continued this day during which time a party of about twenty of the enemy approached a part that happened not to be guarded and about one half of them reached it the rest being drove back by a few Indians who were near the place. The next morning finding it to no purpose to keep up a fire longer upon the fort as we were getting men killed and had already several men wounded, which were to be carried, the Indians determined to retreat and the 20th. reached the Blue Licks where we encamped near an advantageous hill and expecting the enemy would pursue determined here to wait for them keeping spies at the Lick who in the morning of the 21st. discovered them and at half past seven o'clock we engaged them and in a short time totally defeated them.

We were not much superior to them in numbers, they being about two hundred picked men from the settlement of Kentucky commanded by the Colonels Todd, Trigg, Boone and Todd, with the Majors Marling and McGary most of whom fell in the action; from the best inquiry I could make upon the spot, there was upwards of one hundred and forty killed and taken with near an hundred rifles, several being thrown into a deep river that were not recovered.

It was said by the prisoners that a Colonel Logan was expected to join them with one hundred men more; we waited upon this ground to day for him, but seeing there was not much probability of his coming we set off and crossed the Ohio the second day after the action. Capt. Caldwell and I arrived at this place last night with a design of sending some assistance to those who are bringing in the wounded people who are fourteen in number. We had ten Indians killed with Mr. LeBute of the Indian Department, who by sparing the life of one of the enemy and endeavouring to take him prisoner lost his own. To our disappointment we find no provisions brought forward to this place or likelyhood of any for some time and we have entirely subsisted since we left this on what we get in the woods and took from the enemy.

The prisoners all agree in their account that there is no talk of an expedition from that quarter, nor indeed are they able without assistance from the colonies, and that the militia of the country have been employed during the summer in building the fort at the falls and what they call a row-galley which has made one trip up the river to the mouth of the big Miami and occasioned that alarm that created us so much trouble. She carries one six pounder, six four pounders and two, two pounders and rows eighty oars. She had at the Big Bone Lick one hundred men, but being chiefly draughts from the Militia many of them left her on different parts of the river. One of the prisoners mentions the arrival of boats lately from Fort Pitt and that letters have passed between the commanding officer of that place and Mr. Clarke intimating that preparation is making there for another expedition into the Indian country.

We have since our arrival heard something of this matter and that the particulars have been forwarded to you. A detachment of Rangers with a large party of Delawares and Shawnese are gone that way who will be able to discover the truth of this matter.

I am this day favoured with yours of the 6th. August containing the report of Isaac Zeans concerning the cruelties of the Indians. It is true they have made sacrifices to their revenge after the massacre of their women and children some being known to them to be perpetrators of it, but it was done in my absence or before I could reach any of the places to interfere, and, I can assure you, sir, that there is not a white person here wanting in their duty to represent to the Indians in the strongest terms the highest abhorrence of such conduct as well as the bad consequences that may attend it to both them and us being contrary to the rule of carrying on war by civilized nations. However it is not impracticable that Zeans may have exaggerated matters greatly being notoriously known for a disaffected person and concerned in sending prisoners away with intelligence to the enemy at the time Capt. Bird came out as we were then informed.

I flatter myself that I may by this time have an answer to the letter I had the honour of writing to the commander in chief on leaving Detroit.

Mr. Elliott is to be the bearer of this who will be able to give you any further Information necessary respecting matters here.

I am with respect Sir, Your most obedt. and very humble Servant   (Signed) A. McKee

    Shawanese Country, August 28th. 1782. Major De Peyster.

Indorsed 5 1782 From Capt. A. McKee to Major De Peyster, Datd. Augt. 28th. 1782. In Govr. Haldimand's No. 5 23rd. Oct. 1782.

Appendix I

Colonel Daniel Boone to the Governor of Virginia.

(*Virginia Calendar,* Volume 3)

Fayette County, Boone's Station, August 30, 1782.

Sir: A circumstances of affairs causes me to write to your Excellency as follows. On the 16th of this instant, a large number of Indians with some white men, attacted one of our fronteer stations, known by the name of Bryan's Station. The seige continued from about sunrise til ten oclock the next day, then they marched off. Notice being given to the different stations adjacent, we immediately collected 181 horsemen commanded by Colo, jno: Todd: Including some of the Lincoln County Militia commanded by Colo. Trigg, and having pursued about 40 miles, on the 19th instant we discovered the enemy lying in wait for us, on discovery of which we formed our column into one single line and marched up in their front within about forty yards before there was a gun fired: Colo. Trigg on the right, my self on the left, Major McGary in the centre, Major Harlin with the advance party in the front—and from the manner we had formed, it fell to my lot to bring on the attack, which was done with a very heavy on both sides: and extended back the lines to Colo. Trigg, where the enemy was so strong that they rushed up and broke the right wing at the first fire.

So the enemy was immediately on our backs, so we were obliged to retreat with the loss of 77 of our men and 12 wounded. Afterwards we were reinforced by Colo. Logan, which with our own men amounted to 460 Light Horse, with which we marched to the battle ground again. But found the enemy were gone off. So we proceeded to bury the dead—which were 43 found on the ground, and many more we expect lay about that we did not see, as we could not tarry to search very close, being both hungry and weary, and somewhat dubious that the enemy might not be gone quite off, and by what discovery we could make we conclude the number of Indians to exceed 400—now the whole of our militia of this county does not exceed 130.

By this, your Excellency may draw an idea of our circumstance. I know Sir, that your situation at present is something critical. But are we to be totally forgotten. I hope not. I trust about 500 men sent to our assistance immediately, and them to be stationed as our County Lieutenants shall see most necessary, may be the saving of this our part of the country, but if you put them under the direction of General Clarke, they will be little or no service to our settlement, as he lies 100 miles west of us, and the Indians north east, and our men are often called to the Falls to guard them. I have encouraged the people here in this county all that I could, but I can no longer encourage my neighbours, nor myself to risque our lives here at such extraordinary hazzards.

The inhabitants of these counties are very much alarmed at the thoughts of the Indians bringing another campaign into our country this fall, which if it should be the case, will break these settlements. So I hope your Excellency will take it into consideration and send us some relief as quick as possible.

This Sir, is my sentiments without consulting any person. I expect Colo. Logan will immediately send to you by express. By whom I most humbly request your Excellencies answer, meanwhile   I remain, Sir,

Your Excellency's most obedient Humble Servant.

A list of the slain:— Colo. Jno. Todd, Lieuts: Rogers,
     Colo. Trigg,   McQuire,
     Maj: Harlin,   Hinson.
  Capts:—Gordon,   Officers, 10
   " Kincade,   Privates, 67
   " McBride,   ———
   " Overton.   77
          Wounded 12

APPENDIX J.

Hugh McGary.—McGary never himself entered into any written defence of his conduct in this battle. Newspapers in that day were unknown in the State, and his only chance to justify his conduct would be by oral explanation.

Forty years after the battle McClung in his *Sketches* gives the statement of a gentleman who had conversed with McGary as to his part in the action. This gentleman related that he met McGary several years after the battle, at one of the circuit courts, and in conversation McGary acknowledged that he was the immediate cause of the battle, and with great heat and energy endeavoured to justify himself. He asserted that in the council at Bryant's Station the night before the march he strenuously urged Todd and Trigg to await Logan's coming, telling them the Indians would not make a precipitate retreat. He said Todd scouted his advice, claiming that a single day lost would enable the Indians to cross the river and escape; that the time to strike them was while they were in a body; that the talk of their numbers was nonsense, the more the merrier, and that he was resolved to pursue at once, and that there were brave men enough on the ground to enable him to attack with effect.

This nettled him, and he joined eagerly in the pursuit, and when they came in sight of the enemy, and Todd and Trigg began to talk about numbers, position, and Logan, he burst into a passion and cursed them for a set of cowards, and swore that as they had come so far for a fight they should have it, and that they should fight or he would disgrace them; that now it should be shown who had courage or who were d———d cowards, and that he then dashed into the river and called upon all who were not cowards to follow him.

McGary spoke, the gentlemen said, with bitterness of Todd and Trigg, and swore they had received what they deserved, and he, for one, was glad of it.

This story was wisely withheld for forty years after the battle. McGary's subsequent conduct was not such as to restore him to public favour. The atrocious murder of Moluntha in 1786, when with Logan on his invasion of the Indian town in Ohio, stamps him as cruel, base, and brutal, and the declaration that in the presence of their troops he cursed Todd and Trigg and denounced them as cowards will never be credited upon either second hand or firsthand statement of McGary.

The failure to find his name connected in any prominent transaction in the history of Kentucky during his after life is demonstration that his conduct was condemned by those who were his contemporaries.

Appendix K.

Extract of a Letter from Colonel Levi Todd to His Brother, Captain Robert Todd.

(*Virginia Calendar*, Volume 3.)

Lexington, Aug: 26th, '82.

On the 16th instant, in the morning an express arrived from Bryant's Station informing us it was expected a body of Indians lay round the fort. I set off with 30 men to see if it was so, and before I got there (which is five miles distant) was joined by 10 men from Daniel Boones. I found the place surrounded and intended to force our way in. Seventeen of the foremost horsemen rushed in; but being attacked at the mouth of a lane; the remainder, some on horseback, and myself and ten others on foot, were forced to retreat, leaving one man killed, and having three wounded, one of whom died next morning, but the other two will recover.

Our brother being over in Lincoln, I sent expresses there desiring assistance. In the mean time, the Indians made a violent attack upon Bryants Fort and continued it all day and night: and a storm was expected. However they met with some loss, and on the morning of the 17th went off. In the evening, our Brother, Col: Trigg, and Major Macgary came with 130 men. On the morning of the 18th we collected 182 men all on horseback, and pursued the enemy till 8 o'clock in the morning of the 18th, when we got sight of them forming in a ridge in a loop of the river, about three quarters of a mile north of the lower Blue Lick and over the Licking. We had then pursued about 40 miles. We rode up within 60 yards, dismounted, gave and sustained a heavy and general fire.

The ground was equally favourable to both parties and the timber good. The left wing rushed on and gained near 100 yards of ground. But the right gave way, and the enemy soon flanked us on that side, upon which the centre gave way and shifted behind the left wing. And immediately the whole broke in confusion After the action had lasted about five minutes. Our men suffered much in the retreat, many Indians having mounted our men's horses, haveing open woods to pass through to the river, and several were killed in the river. Several efforts were made to rally, but all in vain. He that could remount a horse was well off, and he that could not saw no time for delay.

Our brother received a ball in his left breast, and was on horseback when the men broke. He took a course I thought dangerous, and as I never saw him afterwards, I suppose he never got over the river. Col: Trigg, Major Harlin, Major Bulger, Captains McBride, Gordon, KinKead and Overton fell upon the ground, also our friend James Brown. Our number missing is about seventy-five. I think the number of the enemy was at least 300, but many of the men think five hundred. Colo. Logan with 500 men went to the ground on the 24th, and found and buried about 50 of our dead men. They were all stript naked, scalped and mangled in such a manner that it was hard to know one from another. Our brother was not known.

As people in different parts of the Country will be anxious to know the names of the killed, I will add a list of what I can now remember—

Colo. John Todd, Col: Stephen Trigg—Major Silas Hardin, Major John and Edward Bulger—Captains Wm. McBride, John Gordon, Joseph Kinkead, and Cluff Overton—Lieutenants Wm. Givens, John Kenneday and —— Rogers—Ensign John Mac-Murtry. Privates—Francis McBride, John Price, James Ledgerwood, John Wilson, Isaac MacCracken, Lewis Rose, Mathias Rose, Hugh Cunningham, Jesse Yoeum, William Eadds, Esau Corn, William Smith, Henry Miller, Ezekiel Field, John Folley, John Fry, Val Stern, Andrew MacConnell, James Broown (Surgeon), William Harris, William Stewart, William Stevens, Charles Ferguson, John Willson, John O'Neal, John Stapleton, Dan'l Greggs, Jervis Green, Drury Policy, William Robertson, Gilbert Marshall, James Smith, and Joseph Lindsay.

Appendix L.

Colonel Arthur Campbell to Colonel William Davies.
(*Virginia Calendar,* Volume 3)
Washington County, Virginia, October 3rd, 1782.
Sir: From Colonel Christian and the accounts sent by Major Netherland, the Executive may be fully informed of the State of the War in the Kentucky Country. What if it should be the policy of the British Ministry to drive in from the other side the Apalachian mountain before the signing the preliminaries of peace.

At any rate they are united the savage tribes, and endeavouring to sow the seeds of deep laid animosity, which will lengthen the Indian war to a longer period than most imagine. Nothing now will put an end to it, but a decided blow in the enemy's country, and a peace given them in the hour of their panic and misfortune, afterwards conducted by a proper superintendency, or that Canada becomes ours, or our Allies.

The method of arming and arraying our militia ought to be varied. The bayonet and scymeter must be introduced to enable us now to face the Indians. And evolutions suited to the woods should be learned by both foot and horse. All our late defeats have been occasion through neglect of these, and a want of a proper authority and capacity in the commanding officers. Never was the lives of so many valuable men lost more shamefully than in the late action of the 19th of August, and that not a little through the vain and seditious expressions of a Major McGeary. How much more harm than good can one fool do. Todd and Trigg had capacity, but wanted experience. Boone, Harlin and Lindsay had experience, but were defective in capacity.

Good, however, would it have been, had their advice been followed. Logan is a dull, narrow body, from whom nothing clever need be expected. What a figure he exhibited at the head of near 500 men to reach the field of action six days afterwards, and hardly wait to bury the dead, and when it was plain, part of the Indians were still in the country. General Clarke is in that country, but he has lost the confidence of the people, and it is said become a Sot; perhaps something worse.

The chance is now against General Irvine's succeeding; disappointed in Clark's co-operation, which he was promised, and it is said set out with only 1,200 men. Simon Girty can out-number him; and flushed with so many victories, to his natural boldness, he will be confident.

This state of our Western Affairs calls for the united wisdom and most serious attention of the executive.

The Carolinas are gone on with their expedition against those Cherokees, they say that gives an asylum to Tories.

I wish they may succeed, but still dread the consequence of multiplying our enemies. Two Chickasaw chiefs have been at the Carolina settlement on the Shawanee or Cumberland River, from thence they came to our settlement on Kentucky. Peace are their profession, but complain of our making settle-ment at the Iron Bank, on the Mississippi.

I esteem your person, and like your politicks, therefore send you this communication, merely for your private information.

I am, sir, with usual respect your very humble servant, etc.

Appendix M.

Colonel Benjamin Logan to Governor Harrison,
Giving an Account of the Disaster at Blue Licks.
(*Virginia Calendar,*Volume 3)
Lincoln County, August 31st, 1782.

Sir: I beg leave to present your Excellency and council with one of the most melancholly events that has happened in all this Western Country. On the 14th inst., Captain Holden, from Fayette, pursued a party of Indians who had made prisoners of a couple of boys in his neighbourhood; he overtook them and was repulsed with the loss of four men. On the 16th, a consid-erable army appeared before Bryant's Station, Under the com-mand of the noted Simon Girty, and many other white men; they attacked the station closely, and defeated different parties endeavouring to throw in assistance, but without much loss on our side. An Express was immediately dispatched to Col. John Todd, who at that time was in this County in the neighbour-hood of Col. Trigg.

On the 17th, at night, I received a letter from Col. Trigg, wherein he informed me of what had passed. Orders were im-mediately given for every man to turn out, and on Sunday, the 18th, I crossed the Kentucky with a considerable detachment, and the day after arrived at Bryant's, where I understood the Indians had raised the seige and were followed by Col. John Todd, with 135 of the Lincoln militia under Col. Trigg, and 45 of the Fayette under Col. Bowman. Dreading the consequences that might ensue from this precipitate affair, I immediately pushed within a few miles from Bryant's.

We were met by about 25 men, who informed —— of a total defeat at the Big Blue Licks on Licking. I covered their retreat, and marched back to Bryant's, where I collected 470 men, and the 24th went to the battle-ground and buried 43—our loss in this action is 50 missing from Lincoln, and 15 from Fayette, among whom are Colls. Todd and Trigg (Trigg was quartered), Major Harlan, Capts. McBride, Gordon, Kinkaid and Overton, and Lieuts. Givings, Kennedy, McMartry, Rogers and McGuire, and Mr. Joseph Lindsay, our commissary.

From the situation of the ground, on which our men were drawn up on (the plan whereof I have taken the liberty to enclose) I hardly know how it was possible for any to escape. I am inclined to believe that when your Excellency and council become acquainted with the military operation, in this country, that you will not think them so properly conducted, as to answer the general interest of Kentucky. From the accounts we have received by the prisoners who had escaped this spring, we were confident of an invasion from the Detroit Indians; common safety, then made some scheme of defence necessary; for which purpose, I was called upon by General Clark to attend a council, and after consulting matters, it was determined to build a fort at the mouth of Licking—and shortly I received his orders for 100 men to attend this business, with a certain number from Fayette.

Before the day of rendezvous, I was instructed to send the men to the Falls of Ohio, in order to build a strong garrison, and a row galley, thus by weakening one end to strengthen another, the upper part of the country was left exposed, and the enemy intercepting our designs, brought their intended expedition against the frontiers of Fayette. The immense expenses incurred by the state in this western country, we know is enough to prevent the government from giving us any further aid; but when your Excellency and council are informed that the people have never been benefitted by those expenditures, we still hope your compassion will be extended to a detached, distressed part of your country, as it is not in the power of the people to answer the misapplication of anything by a proper officer.

General Irwin, commanding at Fort Pitt, as a continental officer might probably be more assistance to this country could he receive proper supplies from the state of Virginia, than any other measure that could be adopted—As he has the same enemies to encounter that trouble us, and stores of every kind seem to be of little account to us (ammunition excepted)—Col. Trigg being killed there is a field officer wanting in this county: however I am at a loss how to proceed on the occasion, for all our magistrates have been killed except three; and there can be no court to send a recommendation. Col. Harod formerly acted as a colonel, and who agreeable to seniority ought to have received a commission, is now in being and I think a very proper person for that purpose.

Before I conclude I must beg leave to suggest to your Excellency and council, that a defensive war cannot be carried on with the Indians, and the inhabitants remain in any kind of safety. For unless you can go to their towns and scourge them, they will never make a peace; but on the contrary keep parties constantly in your country to kill; and the plunder they get, answers them instead of trade. Some days past, a white man, one Mr. Simon Burney, with his Indians, arrived at this place in company with two warriors, with talks from the Chickasaws nation—wherein they inform us of their desire to conclude a peace, and the reasons that urged them to war; which was General Clarke's settling Fort Jefferson on their hunting grounds, without consulting them first, and are now enquiring for him.

They own they have done mischief in this, as well as the infant settlement on Cumberland. Should your Excellency and council think proper to hold a treaty with these people, Col. John Donelson, who has before served as an agent for the state is willing to transact any business of that kind.

Since writing the foregoing lines, I have received certain information that Kinchelow's Fort in Jefferson was burned, and 37 souls, made prisoners. Your Excellency and council will please to indulge me a few moments longer, when I take the liberty to add the situation of 470 persons who surrendered themselves prisoners of war to a British officer, then in command from Detroit, with a great number of Indians. As well as I recollect these unhappy people were captured in June 1780. And from authentick intelligence that we have received, they were actually divided in the most distressing manner that could be invented.

Many of the men were taken to Detroit and their wives retained among the Indians as slaves. Some of the men are now at Montreal and others in different parts towards the lakes. As the British were the perpetrators of this cruel piece of mischief. I think by the articles of the Cartel, for the exchange and relief of prisoners taken in the Go: Department, and subsequent measures taken by the different commissioners for that purpose, it is their business immediately to deliver up in this country, at some American post, all the prisoners then taken—or retaliation be had on our part. Unless they are guarded back, they will never get through the Indian country.

I have the honour to be &c. &c. &c. The diagram of the battleground contains the following note:

> The Indians kept the path from Bryants to the Licks, and when Colo. Todd arrived at the top of the hill on this side of the river, the enemy made a shew of about 30 in the bend. Our men marched over upon the hill. The Indians had a very strong line in front which extended from one point of the river to the other. They had flankers and also a party in the rear in order to prevent a retreat. As the river was very deep only at the Licks and the clifts so steep that a passage was impracticable only where they first marched in. thus circumstanced the savages, sure of victory rushed immediately up and threw our men into confusion. What escaped returned mostly by way of the Lick, many were killed after they were made prisoners, as they were seen tied.
>
> From Bryant's Station to the Blue Licks about 40 miles and from thence to the Ohio about 20 or 25. The bent of the river was generally about ½ mile over and from the top of the ridge each way made down small dreans. In these places lay many Indians undiscovered until the attack begun.
>
> It appears near all the warriors on this side of Detroit were on this expedition; some allow 600 or more.
>
> Major Bulger was mortally wounded, and is since dead.

Andrew Steele to Governor Harrison of Virginia.

(*Virginia Calendar*, Volume 3)

Lexington, Ky. August 26, 1782.

Sir. Through the continued series of a seven years vicessitude, nothing has happened so alarming, fatal and injurious to the interest of the Kanetuckians in particular and all its votaries in general, as the present concatination of hostilities, wherewith i am now to acquaint your Excellency.

The fifteenth of this inst: Bryan's Station was beseiged by a number of Indians, whereof I am not able to form a just estimate: the attack continued warm for about thirty hours, during which period, the enemy burned several exterior houses, killed three of our men and made large depredations on the neat stock and crop, they then retired leaving three of their savage party dead on the ground, besides a number circumstantially so.

The seventeenth, we were reinforced from Lincoln, with one hundred and fifty horse men, commanded by Lieut. Col: Stephen Trigg and joined by a few of the Fayette commanded by Col. Jno. Todd, who composed an army of one hundred and eighty two. We followed them to the Lower Blue Licks, where ended the direful catastrophy. in short we were defeated—with the loss of seventy-five men—among whom fell our two commanders with many other officers and soldiers of distinguished bravery. To express the feelings of the inhabitants of both the counties at this ruefull scene of hitherto unparalleled barbarities barre all words and cuts description short.

The twenty fifth, five hundred of the Lincoln militia commanded by Colo. Benjamin Logan (who hitherto had neither been consulted nor solicited to our assistance) marched to the battle ground in expectation of a second engagement, but the enemy had marched several days before, from the order of their march, with many other accruing circumstances, their number was supposed to be nearly six hundred.

Forty seven of our brave Kenetuckians were found in the field, the matchless massacraed victims of their unprecedented cruelty—We are led to conceive that none were captivated, from a number found at the crossing of the creek tied and butchered with knives and spears.

Labouring under these distressing circumstances we rely on your goodness (actuated from a principle of universal benevolence which is the distinguishing characteristic of the truly great and noble soul) that we will not only become the subjects of your commiseration, but of your patronage and protection also, the ballance stands upon an equilibrium and one stroke more will cause it to preponderate to our irretrievable wo, and terminate in the intire breach of our country, if your Excellency is not concerned in our immediate safety—

The Author of this narrative is a person in a private sphere of life and hopes that your forgiving candour, will induce you, to not only pardon the intrusion, but the many inaccuracies that may appear through the whole of this illiterate and undigested detail—as it comes from a welwisher to American liberty and your Excellency's most obedient Honourable Servant.

APPENDIX O.

OFFICERS AND MEN WHO WERE KILLED AT THE BATTLE OF THE BLUE LICKS.

Colonels.

Todd, John,	Trigg, Stephen.

Majors.

Harlan, Silas,	Bulger, Edward.

Captains.

Beasley, John,	Lindsay, Joseph,
Bulger, John,	McBride, William,
Gordon, John,	Overton, Clough.
Kincaid, Joseph,	

Lieutenants.

Givins, William,	McGuire, ——
Hinson, ——,	Rogers, Barnett.
Kennedy, John,	

Surgeon.

Brown, James.

Privates.

Boone, Israel,	Miller, Henry,
Corn, Esau,	Nelson, John,
Cunningham, Hugh,	O'Neal, John,
Eads, William,	Price, John,
Ferguson, Charles,	Polley, Drury.
Field, Ezekiel,	Rose, Mathias,

Folley, John,
Fry, John,
Graham, James (little)
Greggs, Daniel,
Green, Jervis,
Harris, William,
Ledgerwood,
Marshall, Gilbert,
McBride, Francis,
McConnell, Andrew,
McCracken, Isaac,
Robertson, William,
Smith, James,
Smith, William,
Stewart, William,
Stephens, William,
Stapleton, John,
James, Stern, Val.,
Willson, John,
Wilson, John,
Wilson, Israel.

Officers and Men Who Escaped at the Battle of the Blue Licks.

Colonel.
Boone, Daniel.

Majors.
Todd, Levi,
McGary, Hugh.

Captains.
Patterson, Robert,
Johnson, Samuel,
Ellis, William.

Ensign.
McMurtry, John.

Privates.
Boone, Samuel,
Boone, Squire, junior,
Bradford, John,
Cooper, Benjamin,
Craig, Jerry,
Craig, Whitfield,
Field, William,
Graham, James,
Grant, 'Squire,
Hayden, Benjamin,
Harget, Peter,
Kincaid, James,
May, William,
Morgan, James,
McCullough, James,
Netherland, Benjamin,
Reynolds, Aaron,
Rose, James,
Rose, Lewis,
Smith, John,
Steele, Andrew,
Twyman, Stephen,
Wilson, Henry,
Yocum, Jesse.

LEONAUR

ALSO FROM LEONAUR
AVAILABLE IN SOFTCOVER OR HARDCOVER WITH DUST JACKET

AN APACHE CAMPAIGN IN THE SIERRA MADRE by John G. Bourke—An Account of the Expedition in Pursuit of the Chiricahua Apaches in Arizona, 1883.

BILLY DIXON & ADOBE WALLS by Billy Dixon and Edward Campbell Little—Scout, Plainsman & Buffalo Hunter, *Life and Adventures of "Billy" Dixon* by Billy Dixon and *The Battle of Adobe Walls* by Edward Campbell Little (*Pearson's Magazine*).

WITH THE CALIFORNIA COLUMN by George H. Petis—Against Confederates and Hostile Indians During the American Civil War on the South Western Frontier, *The California Column, Frontier Service During the Rebellion* and *Kit Carson's Fight With the Comanche and Kiowa Indians.*

THRILLING DAYS IN ARMY LIFE by George Alexander Forsyth—Experiences of the Beecher's Island Battle 1868, the Apache Campaign of 1882, and the American Civil War.

INDIAN FIGHTS AND FIGHTERS by Cyrus Townsend Brady—Indian Fights and Fighters of the American Western Frontier of the 19th Century.

THE NEZ PERCÉ CAMPAIGN, 1877 by G. O. Shields & Edmond Stephen Meany—Two Accounts of Chief Joseph and the Defeat of the Nez Percé, *The Battle of Big Hole* by G. O. Shields and *Chief Joseph, the Nez Percé* by Edmond Stephen Meany.

CAPTAIN JEFF OF THE TEXAS RANGERS by W. J. Maltby—Fighting Comanche & Kiowa Indians on the South Western Frontier 1863-1874.

SHERIDAN'S TROOPERS ON THE BORDERS by De Benneville Randolph Keim—The Winter Campaign of the U. S. Army Against the Indian Tribes of the Southern Plains, 1868-9.

GERONIMO by Geronimo—The Life of the Famous Apache Warrior in His Own Words.

WILD LIFE IN THE FAR WEST by James Hobbs—The Adventures of a Hunter, Trapper, Guide, Prospector and Soldier.

THE OLD SANTA FE TRAIL by Henry Inman—The Story of a Great Highway.

LIFE IN THE FAR WEST by George F. Ruxton—The Experiences of a British Officer in America and Mexico During the 1840's.

ADVENTURES IN MEXICO AND THE ROCKY MOUNTAINS by George F. Ruxton—Experiences of Mexico and the South West During the 1840's.